FROM THOSE WHO HAVE READ THE BOOK:

"O'Brien soars light years beyond the "business as usual" approach to grant writing. All the world's a stage and O'Brien posits that, to be effective, a grant proposal (like all good writing) should tell a tale. Ingeniously, he demonstrates how the storytelling techniques of Hollywood's top screenwriters can help program planners hone a vague idea into a compelling concept imbued with structure and real-life drama—just the thing to capture the attention of funding agencies. Take this book at its title; it's about making you think smarter, long before you commit a single word to paper. And that's a notion all writers can take to heart."

— Gail Willumsen, Emmy™ award-winning
writer/producer, Gemini Productions

"Being the owner of a research and fund development organization since 1992 and having worked in the nonprofit field since 1980, I know that the material provided in this book will put you many notches above other competitors if you diligently learn and apply what is suggested. This book will help you improve the clarity of your thinking, and therefore, your writing. It will give you a competitive edge in winning grant funding. [It] is brilliant, fun, enjoyable, and easy to read and understand. It is helpful for aspiring and experienced grant writers alike."

— Kristina Brook, MA-Owner, K & M Enterprises,
one of the largest and most successful grant writing
and fund development firms in the nation

"This book is everything I love about Jon's class—honest, insightful, funny and brilliant. It's a great book for all writers."

— Thane Swigart, former student and professional screenwriter

"If you want to know how to do something, listen to someone who has done it. Jon's work has won over $385 million dollars for worthy non-profit groups. In Right Before You Write, Jon shares his unique story-telling approach to writing grants. He's done it. He knows what he's talking about. It would be wise to read and listen since his results have placed him among the top three or four in the nation at his profession."

— Gene Perret, Three-time Emmy™ award-winning
writer/producer and author of Comedy Writing Step-by-Step

FROM THOSE WHO HAVE USED THIS GROUNDBREAKING PROCESS:

"At last…a book that tells you what you really need to know about the art of successful grant writing. The author's experience, passion and humor bring a unique perspective to this book that is filled with practical advice and clear examples. A "must read" for new and experienced grant writers!"

— Cheryl Gourgouris, Director of Programs-Richstone Family Center

"For the past fifteen years Jon has used his planning strategies to breathe life into grant proposals for our organization that nine out of ten times were funded. His unprecedented success comes from first building a relationship with the client, getting to know the internal organization, and studying the specific stakeholders. He then studies the possibilities, sees the potential of the grant, and the effect it will have on the clients and stakeholders. If he decides there is an appropriate match he crafts just the right proposal. Of all the approaches our organization has used to win competitive grants, Jon's approach has been the most unique and most successful."

— Marlene Wilson, Deputy Superintendent-Lennox School District

FROM STUDENTS WHO HAVE TAKEN HIS SCREENWRITING CLASS:

"Taking a class from Jon is like a pat on the back and a punch in the face at the same time. You'll feel like you've just gone ten rounds with the champ, but you'll be grateful for every hit when it's over."

"An off-kilter teaching style that you don't come by a lot."

"This guy knows his stuff, inside and out."

"I have never been more excited to write than when I was in his class."

"Hilarious and inspirational. Best instructor I've had at SBCC."

FROM PROFESSIONALS WHO HAVE TAKEN HIS GRANT CLASS:

"FYI, I'm now two for two on my 'homework' that I've submitted to funders."

"Jon gave us his 'trade secrets.' This willingness to 'give back' to his community is clearly a priority."

"I hope you offer the class again so those unfortunate souls who were shut out can benefit from your experience. When your book comes out, I will be standing in line for an autographed copy."

"I have noticed the improvement in all of my writing, both creative and work related. The '7Cs' were a tremendous help, and one of the key ideas that I absorbed from the class."

"Over the years I have raised close to three million dollars writing grants. Nevertheless, I took something of value from every class. It was by far the most informative grant writing class I have ever attended!!!"

"It related so directly to what I was/am doing. He obviously lives what he teaches (and I do mean lives). Also he went far out of his way to help students outside of class. The nature of his teaching was intensive real-life. I got the feeling, correctly or not, that he was 'giving away' company secrets."

FROM THE CONTRACTUALLY OBLIGATED "ABOUT THE AUTHOR" PAGE

"I consider Jon O'Brien uniquely unqualified to write a book about writing."

Sandy Point Ink LLC
P. O. Box 6847
Santa Barbara, CA 93160
Call Toll Free: 1-866-674-5222
www.SandyPointInk.com
info@SandyPointInk.com

ISBN: 978-0-9816216-0-9
Library of Congress Control Number: 2008902869

Publisher's Cataloging-in-Publication data

O'Brien, Jonathan.
   Right before you write : the groundbreaking planning process used
to win more than $385 million in competitive grant awards / Jonathan
O'Brien, Th.D.
     p. cm.
     Includes index.
     ISBN 978-0-9816216-0-9
1. Proposal writing for grants. 2. Grants-in-aid—United States.
3. Fund raising—United States. I. Right before you write : the
groundbreaking planning process used to win more than three hundred
and eight-five million dollars in competitive grant awards. II. Title.

HG177.5.U6 O27 2008
658.15/224 20—dc22   2008902869

PLEASE NOTE

This book is about a planning process used to win grant monies. Should the
reader require legal or accounting services or advice, it is recommended that a
licensed professional be sought. Although this book is as complete and accurate
as possible, there may be typographical and content mistakes. In addition, this
book contains information on agencies and foundations that is current only up
to the printing date. The author and Sandy Point Ink LLC are neither liable nor
responsible to any person or entity with respect to any loss or damage caused, or
alleged to have been caused, directly or indirectly, by the information contained
in this book. If you do not wish to be bound by the above, you may return this
book to the publisher for a full refund. This book is not endorsed by or affiliated
with any of the programs or agencies referred to herein.

RIGHT BEFORE YOU WRITE

THE GROUNDBREAKING PLANNING PROCESS USED TO WIN
MORE THAN $385 MILLION IN COMPETITIVE GRANT AWARDS

Jonathan O'Brien, Th.D.*

CONTRACTUALLY OBLIGATED ABOUT THE "AUTHOR" PAGE

I consider Jon O'Brien uniquely unqualified to write a book about writing. He is what is known as a literary leper, one who shuns writing classes, touchy-feely writing support groups and at the mention of any self-promotion ducks under his desk and listens to re-mixes of bubblegum hits from the 60s.

At the ripe old age of 25 he managed to doctor up a false ID and worked as a network program executive until, six years later, he turned so ripe he rotted and dropped off that tree.

O'Brien suffers from E.D.D. — Employment Deficit Disorder. Like Forrest Gump (except he has no redeemable qualities, can't run as fast and never earned $678 million at the box office) O'Brien has pinballed from career to career. In fact, when it comes to walking down any one career path, a better name for him might be Forrest Gimp.

Having taught for seven years at juvenile hall (although I swear he served time there instead) he claims to have earned a brown belt in verbal judo. Being somewhat Irish, it wasn't long before he traded in his brown belt for a stiff belt and he hasn't walked a straight line since.

An adjunct instructor at Santa Barbara City College, the student body voted him "Best Role Model From Hell" in nine of the 10 years he has taught there.

As a public speaker and workshop facilitator he is always in demand. After two minutes of hearing him try to speak, the audience demands their money back.

He graduated from UCLA Film School with an MFA (I'd like to tell you what I think the letters M-F-A really stand for) where he received the best education defaulted student loans could buy. After, he earned his honorary *Doctor of Thinkology degree from the universitatus committeeatum e plurbis unum.

"Author" self portrait taken with Photo Booth©

O'Brien once actually tried to cheat the state out of disability by claiming he suffers from B.C.D: Bi-Coastal Disorder. Translated, that means he spends part of the year "working" at his second home on a lake in Maine and the rest of the time living on the Central California coast in proximity to two federal prisons. Coincidence? I think not.

He has two pet peeves (and one pet Ferret named Farrah kept under his bed). His first pet peeve is that he despises those who write glowing third person bios about themselves. As the picture on this page indicates (submitted as Exhibit A, your honor), his second peeve is that he refuses to seriously pose for a picture; a belief commonly held, mind you, by those who purchase do-it-yourself plastic surgery kits and fugitives from the law.

Okay, I'm nearing 500 words, the amount of words as his ghostwriter that I am contractually obligated to write. Yeah, that's right, I said "ghostwriter." Hate to break it to you but do you think O'Brien would actually take the time to write this book? His contribution consisted mainly of showing up just before lunch and sayings thing like, "Put in a few more fancy words."

Okay, now I'm 79 words over. Fat chance O'Brien is going to pay me for these extra words. Fat chance he pays me period.

FOREWORD

Jon and I first met on the telephone in 1997, a couple of days after I gave a radio interview about my relatively new grant writing firm, K & M Enterprises: Research and Fund Development.

Jon happened to have just finished working for a firm that our company had coincidently recently served. In my opinion, working with that firm was rather difficult and I told Jon, "If you worked for that firm…you'll love working at K & M Enterprises." He further cinched the deal with me by regaling me with the story of an exceptional on-the-job experience involving the delivery of a grant proposal barely on time in Boston by sheer force of will, and some extremely creative driving and persuasive taxi-cab techniques. That convinced me that Jon would be an incredible asset to our growing team of writers and researchers.

I was absolutely right. In the 11 years that I have had the privilege of working with Jon, he has never let me down. Not once. His wife once told me how he persevered in film school through the completion of multiple heavy-duty assignments. I would often recall her stories when Jon and I were working together on multiple "all nighters" bailing out new writers who had erroneously thought they had it all together.

Jon is an incredibly capable person and an immensely talented and gifted writer as well. We are fortunate that he has taken the time to write this manuscript.

Right Before You Write provides practical step-by-step advice and exemplary details about how to plan for and write high quality, eminently competitive, and fully fund-worthy grant proposals.

His work is brilliant, fun, enjoyable, and easy to read and understand. It is helpful for aspiring and seasoned grant writers, and offers gems of technique for experienced screenwriters as well.

Writing, and particularly excellent grant writing, can look so easy once you see the final polished product. However, to achieve outstanding writing and results, it takes practice and dedication. Like an Olympic athlete who makes a gymnastic floor exercise look flawless and easy, as well as pleasant to watch, so it is with grant writing — it is a skill and a craft that takes years to learn and even more years to master. Aspiring writers must develop a hunger to be meticulous and detail oriented to win grants. Excellence, not mediocrity, wins grants.

Having worked in the nonprofit field since 1980, and as the owner of one of the nation's largest research and fund development companies, I have had the unique opportunity to work with and cultivate a core team of 25 professional researchers and writers. Serving at the helm of one of the most exceptionally talented teams I have ever known or read about — a team that together has raised more than *$385 million* in grant awards since my company opened its doors in 1992 — I know that the material provided for you in this book will set your work many notches above your proposal competitors *if* you diligently apply what is suggested. This book will help you improve the clarity of your thinking, and therefore, your writing. It will give you a competitive edge in your quest to win and manage grant funding.

So Jon, I thank you for sharing your professional insights with the many people who will read and learn from your book. Thank you also for reminding us why we give it our all to make dreams come true for the less fortunate in the world. It is an honor and blessing to work hard at something that you love to do. Like Jon, my sincere hope is that other writers will seek, and find, the higher calling that drives each of us to greater demonstrations of creativity and excellence in our meticulous and immensely rewarding work.

I have the utmost respect and admiration for all of Jon's accomplishments, and thoroughly anticipate the growth of a vast and multi-disciplinary readership who will sing his praises, as I do, as a result of their own successful application of the writing skills he has so effectively presented for them in *Right Before You Write*. You have my heartfelt congratulations, Jon, on yet another job so well and brilliantly done!

— Kristina Brook, MA
Owner, K & M Enterprises:
Research and Fund Development Services
56659 29 Palms Highway, Suite B
Yucca Valley, CA 92284
760.365.4414 _ KMBROOK@aol.com
May 2008

TABLE OF CONTENTS

Contractually Obligated About The "Author" Page   vii

Foreword   ix

Chapter 1-1 – Edi-Fecal Effigies: RIGHT BEFORE YOU WRITE   1
- Structure, Structure, Structure   2
- Program Design   5

Chapter 1-2 – The Planning Team Approach: SOME OF MY BEST FRIENDS ARE WOOLY MAMMOTHS   9
- ~~Your Grant Writing~~ (no, strike that) Your Planning Team   9
- The Care And Feeding Of Your Grant Writer   10
- The Inverted Pyramid Approach   12
- Responsibilities Of Your Planning Team   13
- "MOST" Planning Teams   15
- The Reader/Scorer   15
- Beware The Grant Gods   16
- Stats Don't Mean A Thing If They Ain't Got That Schwing!   17

Chapter 1-3 – The Program Designers' Bill Of Writes: RIGHT WRITES ITSELF   21
- Your Basic Program Designer's Bill Of Writes Pre-ramble   23

- Ask Not What The Funding Agency Can Do For Your Program, But What Your Program Can Do For The Funding Agency   24
- "Artfully Sell The Problem"   26
- Good Grants Are Read, But Only Excellent Grants Are Funded   26
- "There's No Need To Fear, Underdog Is Here!"   27
- The Main Thing Is To Keep The Main Thing The Main Thing   28
- Better Your Thinking By Asking Better Questions   29
- No Field Ever Got Plowed By A Farmer Turning It Over In His Head   30
- Be Friendly To Your Reader/Scorer And Your Reader/Scorer Will Be Friendly To You   31
- Remember The "Aha!" Factor   32
- Bill of Writes   33
- "Hey Kids!"   34

Chapter 1-4 – Get-Out-Of-Writing-Free Card: DO THINK TWICE, IT'S ALRIGHT   35
- Don't Bother Applying If…   35

Chapter 2-1 – Jon's Almost World Famous Seven Cs! Intro   39
- There I Sat…   39
- Now, Here I Sit…   41
- My Simple Method: Step One   41
- My Simple Method: Step Two   43
- My Simple Method: Step Three   43
- But Don't Confuse Structure With Plot   45

Chapter 2-2 – Character In Movies: THE STAR OF THE SHOW   47
- It's Not WHAT Your Story Is About, But WHO Your Story Is About   47

- The More Dimensional The Character, The More The Audience Will Care About The Character   48
- We Always Root For The Underdog   51
- The Main Character Should Transform From Reactive To Proactive   52

Chapter 2-3 – Character In Program Design: THE STAR OF YOUR PROGRAM DESIGN   53
- Determine Your Target Population   54
- Define Your Target Population   57
- Decide On The Number To Be Served   67
- Delineate Your Target Area   73
- Describe Your Target Population   79
- Review Questions   81

Chapter 2-4 – Crisis In Movies: "A YUCKY MESS"   83
- Crisis And Emotional Depth   85
- Any Good Story Is Told On More Than One Level   85
- The Main Character Should Be Unprepared To Deal With The Crisis   86
- Emotional Wallop   86

Chapter 2-5 – Crisis In Program Design: A RECENT, UNEXPECTED PROBLEM   89
- Don't Confuse Need Indicators With Crisis   90
- "Artfully Selling" The Crisis   90
- The Crisis In Question   91
- What Is The Immediate Crisis That Negatively Impacts Our Target Population?   91
- What Empirical Proof Do We Have That This Crisis Actually Exists?   93
- What Are The Main Causes Of Our Crisis?   94
- Why Did Our Crisis Recently Occur?   95
- How Is Our Target Population's Crisis Local And Unique?   96

- If This Crisis Is Not Immediately And Adequately Addressed, What Are The Repercussions?   97

Chapter 2-6 – The Movie Cuest: THAT'S RIGHT, CUEST WITH A "C"   99
- The Character's Cuest Should Be Tangible, Not Abstract   100
- There Should Only Be One Main Cuest   101

Chapter 2-7 – The Cuest Of Your Program Design: A SIMPLE, SINGLE ENDPOINT   103
- Here's The Good Part   104
- Formulating And Phrasing   104
- The Five Point Overarching Goal Inspection   105

Chapter 2-8 – The Ticking Clock In Movies: MOVIES MUST KEEP MOVING   109
- A Ticking Clock   110
- Types Of Story Clocks In Movies   111
- A Story Clock Should Pass The "Or Else…" Test   111
- The Shorter The Window Of Opportunity, The Better The Clock   113
- The Tick-Tock Hall of Fame?   114

Chapter 2-9 – Clock In Program Design: "WHY NOW AND NOT LATER?"   117
- Do We Have A "Now, Not Later" Sense Of Urgency?   118
- What Is The "Or Else" Factor Of Our Clock?   119
- How Does The Clock, And Or Else Factor, Relate To Our Target Population?   120
- Is Our Clock Realistic?   120
- Back to the Reader/Scorer   121
- Clocking In With Other Examples   122

Chapter 2-10 – Conflict in Movies: NO CONFLICT = NO STORY   125

- Physical Obstacles And Barriers   126
- External Conflict   127
- Internal Conflict   128
- The Simple Equation   129

Chapter 2-11 – Conflict in Program Design: NO CONFLICT = NO GRANT MONEY   131

- A Few Reminders About Conflict   131
- Step One: Brainstorming   133
- Wannabe Example of Step One   141
- Step Two: Weeding Out   145
- Step Three: Grouping and Prioritizing   149
- Step Four: Summarizing   152

Chapter 2-12 – Movies, For A Change: A VISIT WITH PHIL N. LeBLANC   155

- If The Events Of The Story Do Not Change Your Character, Then Change Your Story   156
- Change And That Other "C"   156
- The Ultimate Change Should Be A Result Of The Character's Initiative   157
- A Visit With Our Old Friend, Phil N. LeBlanc   158
- There Will Be Some Changes Made   159

CHAPTER 2-13 – Change In Program Design: A FINISH LINE   161

- Step One: Goals   162
- Step Two: Objectives   166
- Writing The Objectives: Another Wannabe Example   169
- Numbering The Goals And Objectives   174

Chapter 2-14 – Collaboration In Movies: "PACKAGING" 179

Chapter 2-15 – Collaboration In Program Design: A MATTER OF LIFE OR DEATH 181
- First: The Basics   182
- Second: A Little Marriage Counseling   183
- Five Reasons Why A Collaborative Makes Your Program More Efficient   193
- Five Reasons Why Funding Agencies Often Mandate Collaboration   190
- Four Reasons Why A Collaborative Makes Cents   196
- Your Local "Dream Team"   199
- And If You Still Don't Believe Me...   201

Chapter 3-1 – A Great Program Name: YOU'LL KNOW IT WHEN YOU FEEL IT 203
- You'll Know It When You Feel It   204
- Common Characteristics Of A Great Program Name   205
- Pitfalls To Avoid   210
- The Process   211
- My Process   216

Chapter 3-2 – The Hell-evator Speech OR, "I SHOULD HAVE TAKEN THE STAIRS" 223
- Why Hell-evator Speeches Don't Work   224
- A "Little Bit Pregnant" Example   227

Chapter 3-3 – Researching Grants: SHOW ME THE GRANT MONEY! 231
- First Things First   233
- Types Of Grants   235

- Invitations To Apply   238
- Where To Look   239

Chapter 3-4 – Compatibility: DEEP AND IMPORTANT I$$UE$ 247

- In Over Their Programmatic Heads   248
- My Final Answer   250
- Finding The Right Funding Agency: The First Three Steps   250
- Finding The Right Funding Agency: Eligibility Questions   251

Chapter 3-5 – Reading The RFP: THE BETTER THE READER, THE BETTER THE WRITER   263

- Reading An RFP Can Be Frustrating   264
- Back In The Highlight Again   265
- Ask Not What Your RFP Can Do For You, But What You Can Do For Your RF   266
- In One Word: Alignment   267
- If The RFP "Suggests" It, It's In   268
- What Was The Question?   270

Chapter 3-6 – Bidders Conferences: TO GO OR NOT TO GO   273

- Why You Need To Go   274
- "Listen With Hungry Ears"   277
- "Not At Liberty…"   283
- Wearing The Brown Lipstick   285

Chapter 3-7 – Best Practice Models: "RE-IMAGINING"   287

- Choosing A Model   288
- Where To Find Best Practice Models   290

- Specific Questions 293
- Applying What You've Learned To Your Program Design 295

Chapter 3-8 – Epilogue: PROGRAM DESIGN IN A NUTSHELL 299
- Blazing New Trails 302
- And Much Of The Battle Is Internal 303

ACKNOWLEDGEMENTS 305

Index 307

Eye Hear Ya! 316

Chapter 1-1

Edi-Fecal Effigies

RIGHT BEFORE YOU WRITE

Bullshit.

Bullshit inspired me to write this book.

Not very poetic, I know, but true.

I don't mean the one word profanity for nonsense or the slang verb for lying through one's teeth.

I'm talking about the more down to earth variety: cow ka-ka, road apples, prairie muffins, pasture patties.

Some even refer to these fecal land mines as "art."

That's right, art.

Several years ago while on a road trip across country I watched a local Midwest newscast's coverage of an annual cow chip-carving contest. As I watched the proud finalists primp their "artistic" creations, I couldn't help but think: No matter how many creative ways these carvers of crap shape, paint, decorate, and wax lyrical about their edi-fecal effigies, one undeniable fact remained: it was all still ugly, smelly, useless, fly-ridden, common everyday bullshit.

As a screenwriting teacher, program designer and grant writer, I have helped countless writers at all levels of skills and experience shape their work. Most are good and earnest writers, but they're frustrated nonetheless. This is because no matter how dedicated they are and how hard they toil, they fall short when it comes to translating their ideas onto the page.

Why? Because frankly, if what they start with stinks and ain't pretty to look at, it doesn't matter how many creative ways they come up with to shape, rewrite, label, and present their final product, it still has about as much value as the winning entry at the bullshit carving contest.

It's like worrying about the frosting, but not having a cake.

It's like buying great ornaments, but not having a Christmas tree.

It's like choosing the right color, but not having a house to paint.

Okay, before you call the simile police, let me try explaining it this way—

Structure, Structure, Structure

Good writing is good storytelling.

Good storytelling is good structure.

Structure is organizing the main story ideas and elements—before the writing of the plot details. Mastering structure takes years of constant study, application and reflection.

In any decent screenwriting class, one of the first concepts taught is the use of structure to create, or build, screenplays. Despite this, as a screenwriting teacher, the most common questions I get from students on the first day of a new class are not about the essential building blocks of structure but instead:

"How do I get an agent?"

"How much money can I make selling a screenplay?"

And, "Why do you wear such loud, ugly shirts?"

The last question I ignore—can I help it if they have no taste?

The first two questions I refuse to answer. The reason, I tell them, is because too many of them are too eager to reap the benefits of a "hot new screenplay," but are not eager enough to make the time to learn the necessary steps of structuring a story before writing the details of the story.

In *Adventures in the Screen Trade*—one of the best books about screenwriting (one of the best books about writing and the creative process, period)—William Goldman (the first screenwriter to earn one million dollars for a screenplay) writes that the three most important things about telling a story are:

1) Structure
2) Structure
3) Structure

As a foundation is to a building, structure is to a story: the sturdy underpinnings engineered to hold together the weight of all the story details.

What happens to a building if the foundation is not straight and sturdy? It collapses.

What happens when a brick wall is laid and the bottom row and cornerstones are not plum? By the tenth row it's all so uneven it has to be torn down.

What happens when a house is built without a blueprint? Can you say, "Raze it to the ground?"

Same thing when a story lacks structure.

Misguided writers often launch into their story too quickly without taking the time to think it through and plan their basic story structure. Enthusiastic about their original idea, they eagerly write the first 20 pages of their story. Then, sensing that something is wrong and running out of gas, they do a mental Wile E. Coyote™-in-midair-between-two-cliffs double take, take a nosedive, hit bottom, then eventually give up on their project.

Wile E. Coyote™ falls because he has nothing to hold him up.

Writers fail because there is no solid structure to hold up their story. In other words—

They don't get it right before they write.

Most screenwriting books focus too much on the details of writing and selling "hot new screenplays," but not getting the structure right.

Likewise, most grant writing books are about the details: how to write specific responses to specific questions, where to find the grant money, creating budgets, instructions on how to fill in the blanks. But few of those books cover the most important process to address before anything else: strategically planning a program and structuring a grant response to be most effective and competitive, a process called—

Program Design

Program design is a relatively unfamiliar concept to most in the nonprofit world and in grant writing. Here's why:

First, a lot of professionals may hear the term "program design" and say to themselves, "…we're already doing it, we just call it something else…" While not program design exactly, they may call what they're doing:

- Grant development
- Grant research
- Proposal development
- Business plans
- Preparing application materials
- Writing a mission statement
- Cultivating goals and objectives
- Brainstorming workable solutions
- Strategic planning
- Developing a logic model

Second, once many are introduced to the concept of program design they dismiss it as unnecessary—a wasted or redundant step in a process that is already too complex and time consuming.

Third, many program staff of smaller budgeted programs or agencies believe that program design is something only high-priced and unaffordable professional grant writers are hired to develop.

But be warned, in the highly competitive field of grant competitions for grant money, it is becoming more important to outthink your competition.

Program design is not a service or a formula, it's a way of thinking. So, while many may not be able to write as well as an experienced, winning grant writer, anyone can use the same tools and take the same steps they use to outthink and out strategize their competition.

In fact, when grant writers and program planners ask me to help them figure out why they are not winning grants, I usually refuse to read the actual text of their grant proposal. Although they are taken aback, and sometimes even offended, experience tells me that *the root of the problem lies not in their writing, but their thinking.*

In other words, they need to get it right before they write.

Right Before You Write is about this first, and most overlooked, step that must take place *before* the actual writing of your grant occurs. This program design process will take a good or above average grant and structure it into an excellent program design that wins grant money.

To do this, you have to be willing to re-tool your gray matter: that is, reverse engineer the way you think about a grant *before* you start writing a grant.

But first let's agree: sometimes to *think outside* of the box you have to *be outside* of the box.

So, for a little while every day, while you are reading *Right Before You Write*, find time to take your mind off your day-to-day battles. Mentally step outside your agency or program and use the approach in this book to honestly evaluate:

✓ Where your agency or program has been
✓ Where you are now
✓ Where you want to go

American artist Winslow Homer said:

> "...talent is nothing but the capacity for doing continuous work in the right way."

Dedicate yourself to doing continuous work the right way and *Right Before You Write* will help you develop a frame of mind and talent for designing excellent programs *that get funded.*

So, are you ready to take on the task? Willing to make the extra effort? Shoulder the burden? Have you said to yourself, "I can do this!" "I want to do this!" "I must do this!"

Well, you forgot something. Any guesses? Here's a hint in the form of a quote from an obscure author (that would be me):

> "Remember there is no 'I' in team. But there is an 'I' in cliché."

Chapter 1-2

The Planning Team Approach
SOME OF MY BEST FRIENDS ARE WOOLY MAMMOTHS

Designing a program and writing an excellent proposal is a mammoth job, with mammoth responsibilities, under mammoth pressure, fighting mammoth deadlines, against mammoth odds.

And anyone who thinks a grant writer can and should take on a project alone has mammoth brains, the Wooly Mammoth variety—deep-frozen and bound for extinction.

~~Your Grant Writing~~ (no, strike that) Your Planning Team

Instead of working in isolation, a grant writer should be one member of a dream team of local experts and stakeholders involved in each step of the program design process. Depending on your agency's or proposed program's size, your Planning Team should consist of representatives of:

✓ Those who will manage the program and provide services

✓ A far-reaching network of local experts and resources

✓ Collaborating agencies to be involved in the project

✓ The population to be served and impacted by your proposed program

The Care And Feeding Of Your Grant Writer

Whoever came up with the term grant writer as a job description should be banished to purgatory—or worse, forced to read poorly written grants for the rest of eternity.

Actually, the job title "Grant Writer" is probably the second lamest job title ever invented. I think *the* lamest job title might be kindergarten teacher, which I believe translates from German as "…a teacher of kind children in a pleasant garden setting."

Think of all the hats a kindergarten teacher wears: therapist, parenting coach, babysitter, social worker, administrator, musician, artist, writer, linguist, translator, personal trainer, nutrition counselor, fundraiser, referee, custodian, nurse, playmate, art therapist, cook, and lest I forget, soul-shaper of hundreds of children of all backgrounds and abilities.

The term "pleasant garden setting" doesn't quite mesh with all those responsibilities, does it?

Same goes with the job title of grant writer, which I believe translates from German as "…an anal-retentive who has caffeine for blood and will destroy anyone or anything in her/his path to make a deadline."

Here are just some of the hats a professional grant writer wears: meeting facilitator, researcher, program designer, evaluator, needs assessment coordinator, project manager, budget analyst, recruiter, publicist, delivery person, salesperson, mediator, graphic artist, auditor, writer, editor, public speaker, cheerleader and stunt driver (for legal reasons, I won't go into details).

The term grant writer doesn't adequately describe all those responsibilities, does it?

That's not to say that, as a program provider and grant applicant, once you hire a grant writer all you have to do is back up a truck, unload a mess of documents and past grants and leave the writer alone to work her/his magic. If your program or agency intends to design a program and structure a response to a Request For Proposal (RFP) and *then* call in a grant writer simply to write down what you dictate, save yourself some money. You're better off hiring a stenographer.

Remember: a good grant writer should be as much a program designer—that is, part of your Planning Team—as s/he is a writer.

That's important enough to repeat:

**Any grant writer worth her/his weight in White Out®
should be as much a program designer as s/he is a writer.**

11

The Inverted Pyramid Approach

For now, let's view the program design process as an inverted pyramid. At first, the goal is to involve as many people as possible in the initial brain-storming and information-gathering phase. Then, as the clock ticks and the deadline draws near, the number of people involved should narrow, until just a few core people are working on finishing the grant. And finally, the final draft of the response should be the result of one person, one voice: the grant writer. And when the grant is awarded (he said optimistically), the pyramid of involvement should expand from narrow back to wide. This is because, as the program is implemented and spread throughout the community, you're going to need the assistance from all those stakeholders who were involved in the planning.

Responsibilities Of
Your Planning Team

In most cases, especially for smaller or newer programs and agencies, a grant writer is a hired gun: a free-lancer contracted on a per-project basis and not a permanent employee of the program or agency. Therefore, a grant writer is not an expert in your program service area—

S/he only plays one on the blank page.

As part of your Planning Team, the grant writer's primary responsibility should be to get all involved on the same page *and*, at the same time, commit everyone's ideas to paper in a single voice.

The grant writer may temporarily beam down into your universe to walk your walk and talk your talk for six weeks, sometimes as few as six days—okay, I've actually done it in three days—but it's impossible for your grant writer to professionally and personally know the local experts, stakeholders and vital contacts that members of your Planning Team know. Tasks that depend on these relationships, such as asking potential partners to write letters of support, are best left to planning team members who know the community and how it works.

Use of the planning team approach is very efficient. While the grant writer focuses on what s/he does best—turning ideas into a single, persuasive voice on paper—members of your Planning Team can focus on important details and preparatory work such as estimating budgets, researching best practice models, searching for sites to house the program and obtaining signatures on letters and forms.

Sometimes the function of your Planning Team is to pull back on the grant writer's reins. Grant writers have a tendency to promise the moon if it means getting the client money—but that doesn't mean they lie (he said, quickly crossing his fingers). It's just that grant writers are constantly trying to position their project so it stands out from the others. So, while your zealous, desperately competitive, salesperson of a grant writer is more apt to dream up lofty goals s/he *hopes* your planning team might accomplish during program implementation, only veteran program staff on your Planning Team will be able to determine what goals can *realistically* be accomplished.

Excellent program design is also knowing what the funding agency *really* wants, beyond what is stated in the requirements of the grant application package. Often, members of your Planning Team who've worked with funding agency staff on past projects are the only ones with the experience to know this vital information.

The planning team process is also a team building process. The same people who will be responsible for implementing the proposed program will be building working relationships, identifying and addressing challenges, and working out many of the logistics of the proposed program. This will all be done ahead of time, before the grant money and all of the accompanying pressures arrive.

Okay, your eager Dream Team of planning experts is assembled, including the grant writer.

You bought new paper for the flipchart.

You have pens in one hand,
coffee in the other,
donut crumbs on your shirt,
all cell phones are off (yeah right...),
you are all as fired up as your laptops,
and there you sit, staring at the crumbs in the room —
the crumbs of the donuts, that is.

But not so fast. First, some terminology and concepts to keep in mind as you read through this book.

"MOST" Planning Teams

Every story must have an antagonist, a bad guy or an opposing force. In our story, the dark side you want to stay away from is being like M.O.S.T. planning teams. MOST planning teams do not win grants because they are:

M =   Mediocre in their approach.

O =   Obvious in their choices.

S =   Satisfied with less than their best effort.

T =   Timid when it comes to thinking outside the box.

The Reader/Scorer

When you think of the funding agency staff considering your proposal for funding, think of them as the "Reader/Scorer," not just the "Reader."

That's because grant applications are not merely read, but are competitively scored against other proposals from programs or agencies just like yours. Your program will never be judged solely on its own merits but instead on how it measures up against others. Using a rubric, a Reader/Scorer tabulates scores your program design in a number of different categories. These scores are then tallied and compared to your competition.

Although it may be called something nice like "an application process" or "an invitation to apply for funds," make no mistake, grant writing is fiercely competitive.

No mercy. May the best grant proposal—with the highest score—win.

Beware The Grant Gods

I have a pretty good idea of what does and doesn't get funded. Strike that—I have a pretty good idea about what will get *seriously considered* for funding (i.e., what will get you to the final round). After that, the decision is out of our control and in the hands of the Grant Gods. In the preliminary reading/scoring rounds, those vying for grant awards are often anonymous (i.e., any reference to location or names of programs or agency are blacked out). As mentioned before, a rigid scoring system is usually in place and it truly is "may the best grant win." But in the final reckoning round where there are more excellent proposals and qualified applicants than there are grant awards, final decisions are based on factors we applicants have no control over: geographic distribution of funds, political factors, funding agency priorities and the personal preferences of decision-makers. So, just know that, often, even if you write an excellent proposal it may not get funded due to circumstances beyond our control.

What we *can* control is improving the quality of our own applications.

Stats Don't Mean A Thing If They Ain't Got That Schwing!

Okay, so I butchered a great lyric by combining it with a Wayne-and-Garthism, but I'm trying to make you remember a very important point.

A statistic standing alone doesn't mean a thing unless it's compared to another statistic.

Why is this important? Because statistical data is the lifeblood of an excellent grant proposal. It's your job to turn the statistics into a story and to make all your data have meaning to the Reader/Scorer.

For example, MOST applicants in a school-based grant application might write:

> The Generic Unified School District has a high school drop out rate of 28%.

Okay….so?

What is our reaction supposed to be?

28% is merely a number in limbo.

But if they were to instead write:

> The Generic Unified School District has a high
> school drop out rate of 28%, seven times the
> county average of four percent (4%)...

Now that stat has some Schwing! Why? We have something to compare it to. It means something. We know how to react.

Here's another example:

> This is a community where an average of
> 46 vandalism and misdemeanor crimes are
> committed by juveniles per week.

Should we be celebrating or barring our doors? What does the number 46 mean? Let's try it again using a comparative statistic to make it schwing:

> This is a community where an average of
> 46 vandalism and misdemeanor crimes are
> committed by juveniles per week, more
> than three times the amount of any other
> community in the county.

See the difference?

Never assume the Reader/Scorer will make the connection or a comparison. *You* must make the connection for the reader. *You* must make it easy for the reader to understand—to get the point.

Now are we ready to start the program design process? Not quite.

Before we start, it's important that members of your Planning Team take a field trip—one of several to be taken during the reading of this book.

So, shower, shave, floss, clip your permit slips to your shirts, powder your white wigs and put on your Sunday best. We're going to a convention ... a constitutional convention!

Chapter 1-3

The Program Designer's Bill Of Writes
RIGHT WRITES ITSELF

To reiterate, when asked to critique the writing of a losing grant application, seldom do I read the actual text.

First, I ask the applicant about the basic structural elements of their design by having them describe their approach to researching, planning, and thinking about their proposal.

Rarely does a discussion go beyond these points to the specifics of writing the response. This is because what these writers really need to fix is not their writing but their intellectual constitution.

And the greatest constitution in the history of the world has a Bill of Rights, right? So then, a program designer's intellectual constitution deserves the same, right?

So, what follows is a "Bill of Writes" for anyone or any planning team committed to winning more grant money for their program by changing their intellectual constitution, revolutionizing their old approach, and electing to take the quality of their program design to the next level.

Remember, as you read these "Bill of Writes," that how you write is how you think. When you improve your thinking about program design, you will also improve your writing.

Your Basic Program Designer's Bill Of Writes Pre-ramble

Resolved by we program designers and planning team members that in order to establish a new and better way of thinking, adopt a more professional approach, design a more perfect program, submit more excellent grant proposals, ensure our program's fundability and provide for the common good through better program design, we do hereby hold the following truths to be self-evident:

1. Ask Not What The Funding Agency Can Do For Your Program, But What Your Program Can Do For The Funding Agency

This is an important concept that 99% of those new to program design don't understand—nor do 98% of those with some experience. Although 100% of the time this is the concept that means the difference between winning and losing.

MOST applicants try to conform the requirements of the funding agency's grant application to *their pre-existing program* rather than modifying and improving their program services to address the *vision of the funding agency*.

And in any competition, MOST applicants lose.

Keep in mind that the funding agency has an overall plan they intend to implement on a larger scale beyond the scope of your local area. They have invested time, resources, expertise and money putting together this gigantic programmatic puzzle of service organizations with one core purpose—to help realize *their* vision.

The goal of your program design is to become a piece of *their* puzzle. The funding agency is not interested in how you plan to create and solve *your own* puzzle.

Instead, by applying for funds, your Planning Team should demonstrate how and where you will help make the funding agency's vision a reality by making your program a reality.

2. "Artfully Sell The Problem"

In the book, *Entrepreneurial Megabucks: The 100 Greatest Entrepreneurs of the Last 25 Years*, biotechnology pioneer Ronald E. Cape brilliantly described how he generated support and backing. His crusade was to prevail upon others the idea of developing genetic engineering to combat world hunger and incurable diseases. The way he did this can best be described in four words: "artfully selling the problem."

"Artfully selling the problem" also describes the process of program design: identifying a problem (or need) in search of a solution and making that seemingly worst situation seem solvable.

Your program design should impassion and persuade the Reader/Scorer.

In this case, persuade means to sell.

And what are you selling? Not just the fact that your proposed program has a critical need for their support, but that *your proposed program's critical need for grant dollars supersedes that of all the other competing programs seeking support for the same grant dollars.*

Most grants fail to win awards because in addition to not adequately identifying a solvable problem or need, they fail to turn negatives into positives.

That is, they fail to artfully sell the problem.

3. Good Grants Are Read, But Only Excellent Grants Are Funded

We've all heard horror stories about the odds against winning grant awards. Personally, I've won a federal grant competition that issued only nine awards to more than 500 applicants nationwide. Not every grant is such a long shot but you *must assume* it will be extremely competitive. Out of the nationwide competition mentioned above, I'm sure at least 50 were considered "good" grants, but only nine were excellent.

Excellent = funded.

As a grant applicant, you are in a home run derby. Either you hit it over the fence (get funded) or are called out (don't get funded). And a lot of really good grants come up short—some by only a point or two.

But coming up short is unacceptable.

So burn this into your brain's hard drive: the only excellent grants are those that get funded.

Excellence is achieved through a daily, systematic combination of hard work, extra effort, continuing to learn and making sure you want it more than your competitors.

And this is especially important to keep in mind when you're tired, frustrated, want to quit, are looking for someone else to blame and the deadline is encroaching. At that point MOST applicant's attitude is "…let's just get this over with…"

But instead, that is the exact moment in time where your attitude should be, "What can I do to make our good program design excellent?"

4. "There's No Need To Fear, Underdog® Is Here!"

"When in this world the headlines read of those whose hearts are filled with greed who rob and steal from those who need to right this wrong with blinding speed goes Underdog! UNDERDOG!"

Remember the late 1960s cartoon show Underdog®?

Not a bird, nor plane, nor even frog—but little old Underdog? Underdog featured a very unlikely champion of justice: a small Beagle with a wimpy voice (Wally Cox) in a baggy, ill-fitting costume. He was always outnumbered and outwitted. Yet we always rooted for him to win.

Why? We all root for the underdog.

What does any dictionary say about an underdog? Something like, "...a person or group that, despite their best efforts, is expected to lose or not be given a fair chance because of injustice, discrimination, etc."

But, an underdog is not someone who rolls over and surrenders.

Instead—and this is why we root for an underdog—the underdog has the *will and desire* to change for the better.

So turn those who will benefit from your proposed program (your Target Population) into an underdog that the Reader/Scorer will root for because, despite the odds, they have the *will and desire* to overcome the obstacles they face and change for the better.

5. The Main Thing Is To Keep The Main Thing The Main Thing

Too often, the program design process ends up as a series of compromises with several factions wanting to get their own pet project or staff position funded to the exclusion of other pet projects or staff positions. Discussions are reduced to a series of tradeoffs until a project is patched together: stick a part of this over here, throw in a little of this program so so-and-so won't gripe, gotta put this in or so-and-so is threatening to pull out.

The result is a Frankenstein's monster of a program design—heartless, soulless and destined for self-destruction.

It's important that your Planning Team fight the same crusade, under one flag, for the same cause: *the overarching goal* of your Planning Team's proposed program. The overarching goal is that *simple, singular main thing* that you want your proposed grant-funded program to help your Target Population achieve.

So don't confuse your proposed program's *specific* overarching goal with your agency's existing mission statement.

When the main thing is "keeping the main thing the main thing" for all involved, it's remarkable how each idea or a component either falls into place or is weeded out.

What results is a clear, simple, singular, focus in your program design—your program's overarching goal.

6. Better Your Thinking By Asking Better Questions

George S. Patton once said, "If everyone is thinking alike, then somebody isn't thinking."

Here's something else to remember: If you always do what you always did, you'll always get what you always got.

Questions that begin with "What if...?" and "Why can't we...?" and "How about we try..." are springboards to innovation. The momentum from meetings where these questions are posed in a non-threatening, egoless, environment can be inspiring.

It's not unlike how great sports teams, at any level, describe those blissful moments of competition when they temporarily achieve another level of consciousness and meld together as a single unit to achieve as a team what no individual can.

No one knows where the next great idea is going to come from. It doesn't matter, as long as those at the meeting are thinking about bettering the program and not their personal agendas.

If these outside-the-box questions are aligned with the themes of "What are other programs doing and how can we make our program better than theirs?" and "How can we do it in a way that's never been done before?" and "What's best for our Target Population?," then your Planning Team is taking a big step toward bettering your thinking by asking better questions.

7. No Field Ever Got Plowed By A Farmer Turning It Over In His Head

This is a common saying in Maine, but every region in the country seems to have its own version.

Coming up with a great idea is only the first step in the process. A fearlessness to roll up your sleeves and have the energy, courage and perseverance to see the idea through is the real journey.

Those who are easily satisfied by their mediocre work (i.e., want to take the easy way) are "Type L" Personalities:

"L" as in lazy.

You know the "Type L": 9 to 5 are not the hours they work but the odds that they'll fall asleep in the next meeting.

When opportunity knocks on the "Type L's" door, they put out the DO NOT DISTURB sign.

Instead of being a "Type L" take a more professional approach: no shortcuts, no settling for "that's good enough," always do more than the minimum requested by the funding agency and do your homework better than anyone else.

As Mark Twain said:

"Ideas are funny little things. They won't work unless you do."

8. Be Friendly To Your Reader/Scorer And Your Reader/Scorer Will Be Friendly To You

So, how will your program design stand out from the hundreds of other applicants in the competition?

One way is to make it Reader/Scorer-friendly. As mentioned before, when thinking of the funding agency staff considering your proposal for funding, think of them as the "Reader/Scorer," not just the "Reader." That's because grant applications are not merely read, but are competitively scored against other proposals from programs or agencies just like yours.

In two words, Reader/Scorer-friendly means: be compelling. In Latin, compelling translates as "drive and together." In other words, connect and present the elements of your design in a way that is so irresistibly interesting and unique—even captivating—that your Reader/Scorer wants to brag to another Reader/Scorer, "Look at the jewel I found!"

And remember, Reader/Scorers are not Scantron™ machines. They're human beings who are highly vulnerable to one very infectious emotion—passion.

On the other hand, if your proposal has every indication that you really don't care—misspellings, improper margins, sloppy mistakes, lazy writing, boilerplated, uninspired—then why should the Reader/Scorer care?

Artie Shaw said it about jazz, but the same principle applies to a Reader/Scorer-friendly program design:

"If it moves you, it's going to move others."

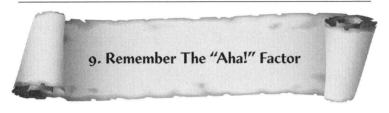

9. Remember The "Aha!" Factor

"Woke up this mornin' feelin' fine
There's somethin' special on my mind
Last night I met a new girl in the neighborhood,
Whoa yeah,
Somethin' tells me I'm into something good."

—Herman's Hermits

In one word—goosebumps.

I can't possibly tell you the physiological reason we get goosebumps other than it has something to do with a molecule called PEA (Phenylethylamine), a kind of natural amphetamine that revs up the brain and the central nervous system.

All I know is, embrace that "…something tells me I'm into something good…," "Aha!" feeling whenever you get it and then apply it to your program design.

Just when the Reader/Scorer has thought s/he has heard it all, your application presents a detail or a thought or a program component that is new to her/him. Their response?

"Aha!"

And let's not forget the universally understood symbol used to represent what happens when the Reader/Scorer also experiences your "Aha!" factor:

BILL OF WRITES

Resolved by we grant writers and program planners that in order to design a more perfect program, write more excellent proposals, use a more professional approach, establish a new and better way of thinking, ensure our program's fundability, and provide for the common good through better programming—we do hereby hold these truths to be self evident:

1. Ask not what the funding agency can do for you, but what you can do for the funding agency.

2. "Artfully sell the problem."

3. Good grants are read, but only excellent grants are funded.

4. "There's no need to fear, Underdog is here!"

5. The main thing is to keep the main thing the main thing.

6. Better your thinking by asking better questions.

7. No field ever got plowed by a farmer turning it over in his head.

8. Be friendly to your Reader/Scorer and your Reader/Scorer will be friendly to you.

9. Remember the "Aha!" Factor

Chapter 1-4

Get-Out-Of-Writing-Free Card
DO THINK TWICE, IT'S ALRIGHT

Right about now, you may be having second thoughts about designing an excellent program. It is a daunting process—the pressures, decisions, relentless debates, last-minute complications, heated negotiations over costs —

And that's just when your Planning Team orders lunch!

Remember in the game Monopoly© those two "Get-Out-Of-Jail-Free"cards? Program design has an equivalent. There are some instances where you shouldn't even bother working on a program design because it would be a waste of time submitting and not seriously considered for funding.

Don't Bother Applying If ...

The following points will be explained in greater detail in subsequent chapters. There are some exceptions to these rules of thumb (as determined by the requirements of each individual grant or funding agency). But in general, don't bother applying if:

- You are requesting funds for capital to build or remodel buildings or buy real estate.
- You are an individual requesting grant funds to perform whatever good deed you're doing.
- You are applying as an individual agency and your program *has not* been operating for three years with at least one full-time staff.
- You've been operating for at least three years and *do* have at least one full-time staff, but have not been externally audited.
- Your program or agency is seeking grant funds as a reward and recognition for on-going meritorious service your program provides to the community.
- You've never read an example of a winning grant in the same program area and budget range.
- You seek support to *solely fund* on-going operating expenses for your agency and/or a current program.
- You seek to replenish funds because your existing agency/program experienced unexpected cost overages due to poor management.
- You intend on cutting and pasting from one of your old proposals to apply for a new proposal.
- You don't plan on attending the funding agency bidders' conference because you have applied for a grant from them before.

- Your program or agency intends to apply as a single agency without any other expert, program or agency involved as a partner.
- You seek funds to support an idea for a *new* non-profit organization that you're in the process of forming.

+ + +

Again, if any of the above describes you or your program, I strongly suggest you *do* think twice and redeem your "Get-Out-Of-Writing-Free" card.

If not, then you're ready to get it right before you write, right?

It's time to roll up your sleeves and get down to the serious business and hard work involved in program design.

Got popcorn?

Chapter 2-1

Jon's Almost World
Famous Seven Cs! Intro

There I Sat ...

Five weeks into a 10-week graduate seminar at UCLA's prestigious film school and I didn't have a clue. I was lost, confused, doubting myself—the projector was running but my bulb was not on.

No matter how many different ways the professor tried to fervently explain the abstract concept, the more my chances of grasping the complex subject slipped away.

The subject? Structure in film—very important stuff for us to understand. How did I know that? The instructor kept telling us it was "...very important stuff for us to understand." Structure is the lifeblood of all good stories, he would implore.

But I didn't get it.

Structure seemed like an impossible concept to wrap my head around—like trying to absorb a foreign language by learning all the new words at once. Why was structure so important? I had studied hundreds of movies up to that point but had no idea how I could possibly apply this "important stuff" to what I was doing.

And then one day, I got it.

Don't ask me how. I'd do anything to remember which switch was flipped that started the logic juice flowing, but I can't. All I know is the concept of structure—and its importance not just in movies or storytelling but also in everything—suddenly fell into place.

In my mind, I danced around the film department like Gene Kelly in *Singin' In The Rain*—What a glorious feeling, I'm happy again! I'm laughin' at clouds! I'm structuring in the rain!!!"

Structure IS the lifeblood, of everything, everywhere:

- Our bodies have structure—our skeletal system!
- Songs are structured—the 32-bar AABA form!
- The life of a butterfly is structured—the stages of metamorphosis!
- Buildings are structurally engineered—cornerstones, arches, support beams!
- Football is structured—the opening kickoff, two halves and a halftime!

How could a subject that at first seemed so complex and impenetrable now be so simple to understand? I made a vow then and there, "As God [was] my witness" (we were film school brats, we always used movie quotes), that if I ever taught or wrote about film or screenwriting or storytelling, that I would find a way to make structure accessible, easy to understand and easy to apply to real world situations.

Now, Here I Sit ...

...an ex-television network program executive who used structure as a tool to develop movie ideas, a professional storyteller who has used structure to pay the rent for many years, a writing and screenwriting instructor who has also taught a variety of film courses that included units on structure, a radio host who tightly structured each of his broadcasts, and a successful grant writer who specializes in helping nonprofits win the big bucks with program design (another name for structure). Now, I'm trying to put down in words the method/s I have used to teach structure so that others may benefit.

I thought understanding the basic principles of structure was hard, but teaching those principles is even harder.

This is especially true because I subscribe to Louis A. Berman's theory that a good teacher should, "...strive to be a master of simplification and an enemy of over simplification."

My Simple Method: Step One

The first step in helping students understand structure is to help them recognize that structure is an essential ingredient in all forms of storytelling.

Joseph Campbell, in his masterwork on mythological storytelling, *The Hero With A Thousand Faces*, identified a universal structure in mythological tales that he simplified into 12 basic steps. His theory was that while appearance, setting, language, message and religion of the hero/heroine in the world's disparate classic stories may differ, the basic steps of each story (what he called *The Hero's Adventure*) remain the same. It's these basic storytelling steps that have worked for centuries and are still used today by modern mythmakers—screenwriters and filmmakers.

Fables and fairy tales told at bedtime have been passed down from generation to generation for thousands of years. Why? Because they all contain certain common structural elements that make them great stories. Most start with a variation of "Once upon a time..." and end with a variation of "...they lived happily ever after."

One of the last things Walt Disney, a master at retelling these classic tales, said was, "...of all the things I've ever done, I want to be remembered as a storyteller."

And Disney incorporated structure into more than movies. Think about the structure of Disneyland where Disney wanted us to feel like we are walking into a movie. It's no accident that from the moment we buy our ticket to the time we enter through the darkened Main Street tunnels that the entry is like a movie theater lobby—turnstiles, coming attractions posters, the smell of popcorn. And it's no coincidence that the two tunnels at the entrance are built very closely to the aspect ratio of a movie theater screen. Because of this, we actually get the feeling that we're walking into a movie—another world. And, Disney pioneered the concept of amusement park rides that not only thrill but also tell a structured story with a beginning, middle and end.

My Simple Method: Step Two

My second step is to help students explore how story elements are organized through structure within something they know well and love—movies.

The movie *For The Love Of The Game* is a story about a pitcher looking back at his life in nine distinct phases that parallel a nine-inning baseball game.

Three Days Of The Condor is structured around the three desperate days a bookish CIA agent has to find out why everyone he once trusted is now trying to kill him.

In *Apocalypse Now*, the spine (another word for structure) of the story is the river Willard follows that carries him to a final apocalyptic confrontation with Colonel Kurtz.

My Simple Method: Step Three

My third step is to help grant writers and staff of non-profit agencies and programs connect the principles of structure in storytelling with program design.

It's a match made in structural heaven.

Why? Storytelling is simply one human being communicating with another on an emotional level.

Likewise, a well-designed program and well-written grant proposal reaches out to the Reader/Scorer and pushes her/his emotional buttons.

So, that's what you need to accomplish when you design your program—you need to structure a good story.

And what makes up the basic building blocks of a good story? Well funny you should ask. There's something I oh-so-modestly call:

Okay ...maybe not so modestly.

Jon's Almost World Famous Seven Cs! have been tried out and tested on hundreds of screenwriting students, high school and college students, grant writers and program providers. They have even been used by juvenile hall creative/therapeutic writing classes where *Jon's Almost World Famous Seven Cs!* allowed incarcerated youth to escape — no, not *that* type of escape.

So, why the name *Jon's Almost World Famous Seven Cs!*?

The majority of well-told stories—no matter what the format, form, or audience—have within them common structural elements that all happen to begin with a "C."

These common elements are also known as story structure—major building blocks that organize the story and give it a direction and focus that entices the Reader/Scorer through to the end.

But Don't Confuse Structure With Plot

Screenplays are structured using three, 30- and 60-page blocks of action called acts. These acts are further broken down into smaller 10-page blocks of actions called sequences. Another structural essential of a screenplay is the building up to a big resolution in the third act of the story that is emotionally cathartic for both the characters in the movies and the audience watching. This type of finale is often called a "big event", the "set piece" or, if you really want to sound like a pompous film student, "deus ex machina."

On the other hand, plot is what a writer writes *after* the structural work. Plot is the finer details: the step-by-step progression of emotional events that happens to the characters along the way, dialogue, character revelations, plot twists and other storytelling devices like backstory.

Like movies and other stories, your program design needs structure too. The basic program design is the structure—the writing of the details in response to specific RFP questions is like writing the plot.

So, in this second section, as I do with my screenwriting students, I'll explain each of *Jon's Almost World Famous Seven Cs!* by using examples from the most popular form of storytelling today; movies. I'll also explain a number of axioms and tricks of the screenwriting trade.

Then, I'll help your Planning Team apply those principles to your program design.

So, now ...on with the show!

Chapter 2-2

Character In Movies
THE STAR OF THE SHOW

SCREENWRITING AXIOM #1

It's Not WHAT Your Story Is About, But WHO Your Story Is About

Remember watching the movie *Titanic*? When the ship began to sink did the audience in the theater cry over all the steel girders and fine silverware gone to waste? No. What audiences really cared about was what happened to the *characters aboard the ship*—not the ship.

The goal of any good storyteller worth their weight in overdue library books is to create an immediate and lasting image of exactly WHO the story is about, so the audience thinks to themselves, "Yes, I know who that person is" and "Yes, I care what happens to that person," or "That person could be me."

The more the movie audience connects with and relates to a character on the screen—the more they root for and care about what happens to that character.

"Where else does an event take place but in people, really?" said Elia Kazan, winner of two Academy Awards® and three Tony Awards®, whose emotionally powerful directing (e.g., *On The Waterfront, East Of Eden, A Streetcar Named Desire,*) focused on the inner turmoil of characters. "You have external things, but the event, the drama, as I see it, takes place within people."

SCREENWRITING AXIOM #2

The More Dimensional The Character, The More The Audience Will Care About The Character

One of the first lessons taught in any decent screenwriting class is that it is not enough to just *describe* a main character; a character must also *develop* throughout the story.

Over the course of a movie, a main character comes to life before our eyes much like a photographic image slowly appears in a tray of developer in a darkroom. This occurs as a result of the unfolding events and conflicts within the story, interaction with other characters, and revelations about the past.

"The body is a house of many windows," wrote Robert Louis Stevenson. How a character responds to other characters and obstacles provides the audience with different and unique windows into the psychological complexity of the main character.

The goal is to make the audience understand and empathize with (understand and share the feelings of) a character.

Screenwriters use a variety of techniques to develop a character. One is environment. A character not only shapes, but also is shaped by, the world around them. Writers will make a concerted effort to make the character's environment reflect and comment on a character's personality.

Think of the movie *Sideways* and the apartment of the main character, Miles. Describe the interior of his apartment and its *haphazard* decoration, *glum* color and *beat up* furniture and you're also aptly describing Miles' personality.

Switching universes, think of Ben Kenobi's dwelling in *Star Wars*: spartan, comforting, secure, a calm, quiet retreat—all the feelings you associate with the Jedi Knight who lives there.

Take an objective look around the office or room where *you* work. What does it say about you (other than you should have probably hired a maid service three weeks ago)?

Why do Manhattanites idle higher than, say, their lower key neighbors from a small fishing village on the northern coast of Maine? Because of their geographic and socio-economic context—their environment. The robust city is like an IV of adrenaline; the seaside calms and humbles.

Other devices writers use to develop characters include:

- **Adversity:** A character is defined by how they deal with (or don't deal with) adversity and obstacles and other characters in the story.
- **Power:** Each character has a certain ability or power unique to them, some positive trait that they

can capitalize on in the story. For some it might be political power. For others: charisma, fortitude, sexual, fear or money.

- **Sacrifice:** Hero is a Greek word that means, "to protect and serve." If a character is going to be a true hero, s/he will sacrifice her/himself for the greater good of others.

- **Motivation:** The word motivation is derived from the Latin word "movere," meaning "that which inwardly moves a person to behave a certain way." In movies, motivation is what drives a character to take action. Most stories are launched when a character declares they are "tired of talking about it," or "tired of waiting for something to happen" or have "nowhere else to go." By taking action they are willing to do whatever it takes to change their lives for the better.

- **Point-of-view:** To understand a character, the audience must also understand the character's point-of-view. How a character talks, acts, thinks, sees, reacts toward others, and their beliefs and experiences are filtered through their unique attitude/outlook toward the world.

- **Backstory:** To develop a good character, a writer needs an in-depth knowledge of that character's backstory including significant life shaping events, cultural influences, and a sense of their history.

SCREENWRITING AXIOM #3

We Always Root For The Underdog

What does the dictionary say about an underdog? Mine says: "Stop reading this dictionary and go watch the movie *Rocky*."

Rocky is a classic underdog story about a kind-hearted, second-rate loan shark with a chance to "not just be another bum" by fighting for the heavyweight title. The movie poster reads something like "...his entire life was a million-to-one shot."

In the Bill Of Writes chapter, an underdog was defined as a person or group that is expected to lose or miss out, but they have the will and desire to improve their conditions and way of life despite the odds against them.

In movies, we like to watch an underdog of a character—pitted against supposedly insurmountable odds and redoubtable antagonists—achieve the seemingly impossible:

- A clerical worker, representing the ill and indigent, takes on a utility company in the costliest lawsuit in history. She might not have a legal background or trial experience, but she knows she's right.
- A loser son charged with resurrecting his recently deceased father's business might be sheltered, inexperienced and disrespected by the older workers. But now he is willing to risk his own fortune to prove himself by rescuing the business and his father's good name.

- An untested caddy tees up against the world's greatest golfer in the U.S. Open. He may be a long shot but he has a love for the game and a special gift to see it in ways no one can imagine.

SCREENWRITING AXIOM #4

The Main Character Should Transform From Reactive To Proactive

Or, as the wise and great old philosopher, Popeye©, used to say before taking control of his life and beating the brute out of Brutus, "I had all I can stands and I can stands no more!"

In most movies the main character creates or controls a situation by *causing* something to happen, rather than *reacting* to it after it has happened. S/he may be assisted and supported by others in some way, but for a story to be good, it has to be the main character who finds strength and summons up the will and desire to change.

To take the outcome of the story out of the hands of the main character and have her/him sit on the sidelines and watch the results is a major no-no of screenwriting and storytelling.

✛   ✛   ✛

Backstory, point-of-view, will and desire to change, products of their environment, underdog—let's see how these methods of developing a character relate to your program design.

Chapter 2-3

Character In Program Design
THE STAR OF YOUR
PROGRAM DESIGN

The storytelling principles of developing the "main character" can be applied to your program design. However, instead of "main character," refer to the specific group of people who will benefit from your proposed program services as your TARGET POPULATION.

After your Planning Team accomplishes the following five tasks in this chapter, both your Planning Team and the Reader/Scorer will have a clearer picture of your Target Population.

    Task #1:   Determine your Target Population

    Task #2:   Define your Target Population

    Task #3:   Decide on the number to receive services

    Task #4:   Delineate your target area

    Task #5:   Describe your Target Population

TASK #1
DETERMINE YOUR TARGET POPULATION

When you apply the first axiom about characters (it's not WHAT, but WHO your story is about) to your program design, then the very first question your Planning Team asks *should not be*, "What services will our program provide?", but instead:

"WHO will we provide services to?"

Your design isn't about a program. It's about PEOPLE receiving services within the program.

Your design isn't about a building. It's about PEOPLE within that building benefiting from services.

Your program isn't about helping the east or west side of a town. It's about helping PEOPLE who live in that area.

Your program isn't about a school. It's about supporting STUDENTS who learn, and STAFF who teach, there.

Your program is not about the non-profit you're trying to start or a political movement, it's about the PEOPLE who will benefit from those causes.

Start this process of determining your Target Population by deciding WHO you are helping, in very general terms at first.

Let's use the design for an after school arts program as an example.

Remember: it's not about the school, it's about WHO in the arts program will benefit. In other words, what specific group within the school will directly receive the proposed services? The logical choice to benefit from an after school arts program would be students.

In other types of programs the choice may not be as obvious. For example, in a gang violence prevention program there could be at least four other specific targeted populations that might benefit from services:

1) **Parents,** by being educated about the problem and accessing support resources to reinforce school prevention activities in the home.

2) **Teachers,** by receiving additional training to identify gang behavior and implement a new prevention program within the school curriculum.

3) **Bullies,** by understanding why their acts of name-calling, harassment and physical assaults have been identified as a national public health concern and a precursor to gang involvement.

4) **Students,** from positive alternative activities, role models and prevention counseling.

Often, planning teams will ask, "Can we have more than one Target Population?" The answer is no. While a number of specific groups may benefit from the services of your program, *focus on one Target Population.* Remember that the purpose of narrowing down your Target Population to one specific group is so your program can be more focused on the specific problems, and the specific solutions, of a specific group. This focus results in the services delivered being more efficient, economical and customized to your Target Population.

Take My Example ... Please

Let's take a look at how applying the first character axiom ("...not what but who...") might improve your program design by determining your Target Population. Had they not read these first chapters about the first "C" in program design— CHARACTER—the planning team of the hypothetical *For Example Arts After School Program* might make the mistake of describing their Target Population like this:

Version One: The *For Example Arts After School Program* is designed to provide a much needed arts program to the Generic School District.

Version one reads as if the intention of the grant is to provide services to a district, which is nothing but a bunch of buildings. Remember, we care more about the students inside the buildings than we do the buildings.

So, if we were to improve Version One, we would ask ourselves, in very general terms at first, to whom will we provide services? In this example, the answer:

Version Two: The *For Example Arts After School Program* is designed to provide a much needed arts program to students of the Generic School District.

Better, but not excellent. There's still more work to do.

But, by completing Task #1, we've determined a specific group who most need, and will most benefit from, the proposed services. Now let's continue with step two of the process to develop (i.e., create a picture) of this Target Population in the Reader/Scorer's mind.

TASK #2
DEFINE YOUR TARGET POPULATION

Remember the Character Axiom, "The More Dimensional The Character, The More The Audience Will Empathize With The Character?" The goal was to motivate the audience to understand and empathize with the main character. In screenwriting, this process is called "developing" the main character.

For program design, let's think of it as DEFINING your Target Population. Your Planning Team does this by asking:

What Are Four NEED INDICATORS
That Define Our Target Population?

Need indicators can also be referred to as "criteria," "descriptive elements," "population profiles," "risk factors" or "indicators."

I prefer the term "need indicator" because it truly defines the purpose of these descriptive phrases.

MOST applicants are satisfied with using one or two need indicators. Excellent grant proposals use *at least four* need indicators to define their Target Population.

Here are some indicators the planning team for the *For Example After School Arts Program* might use to more narrowly define their Target Population: age range, grade levels, grade point average, academic performance, poverty level, gender, ethnicity, length of time living in the target area, criminal behavior, family situations (e.g., children from single-parent families, home life and any number of other risk factors).

The number of Target Population indicators can be infinite. But with the limited space allotted in proposals, all of them cannot be used.

So how do you decide which indicators to use? Remember a key factor here:

They should be thought of as NEED indicators, not just indicators.

What that tells you is to use a need indicator that narrows your specific Target Population AND creates their need for support. Don't let this concept slip by. It is critical to your program design:

Your Planning Team's job is to "artfully sell the problem" by putting the NEED in your Target Population's need indicators.

Take the *For Example After School Arts Program*. We know that their Target Population is "students," but that proposed Target Population is too generalized.

There is no need in their need indicator/s.

So let's improve it.

Let's say that, due to forced budget cuts, the district recently eliminated the entire arts and music budget for grades 5–6. Now, students in grades 5–6 are the only students in the district with no arts and music programs. Again, we didn't just pick this need indicator arbitrarily. We will "artfully sell the problem" by turning the indicator into a NEED indicator.

With this in mind, MOST applicants might be satisfied with this version:

Version Three: The *For Example Arts After School Program* is designed to provide a much needed arts program to 5–6th grade students of the Generic School District whose arts and music education budget was recently eliminated because of budget cutbacks.

Better still, but not yet excellent.

We still haven't developed a true picture of these 5–6th grade students. Watch what happens when we use three more need indicators to bring the total to four and better develop the Target Population:

2nd need indicator: A high percentage of these 5–6th grade students' families qualify for free-/reduced-cost lunches and have no financial means to access this education elsewhere.

3rd need indicator:	A majority of these 5–6th grade students are on academic probation (i.e., at risk of being held back a grade) because they are unmotivated to attend school.
4th need indicator:	Though a majority of these at-risk 5–6th grade students have the greatest number of mental health and socio-economic risk factors of any elementary students in the district, there is no safe harbor for them in the community after school, during the high crime time of 3–6 p.m.

See the difference when you marry an indicator with a need?

For example, one need indicator of this Target Population is that they are unmotivated. Their need? Something to motivate them and get them interested in school so they can get back up to grade level.

Another need indicator is that they have a number of risk factors that could lead to negative behavior, especially if after school their lives are unstructured and unsupervised. The need? Supervision, structure and guidance after school.

Marrying the need with an indicator further develops the picture of the Target Population:

Version Four: The *For Example Arts After School Program* is designed to provide a much needed arts program to 5-6th grade students of the Generic School District who have no access to arts and music education at school because of recent district budget cutbacks. These 5-6th grade students are the poorest and most at-risk students in the district who have no structure or supervision at home during the high crime time of 3-6 p.m. These students are also performing poorly in school because they are unmotivated and suffer from poor attendance.

Compare version four to version one. Not bad, not bad at all.

But, we're *still* not done.

Target Population Characteristics

Coming up with four need indicators is the equivalent of properly framing the composition of a photo. Now it's time to work in the layers of shadings, textures and details of the image until what's truly unique about your Target Population emerges. Keeping in mind how screenwriters develop their characters, think about and research your Target Population and ask yourself similar questions:

What Is Your Target
Population's Backstory?

How did they get where they are? What socio-economic conditions came into play to put them in a position where they need assistance?

The hypothetical *For Example Arts After School Program* may operate within a port-of-entry community with a population that is 95% Hispanics and Latinos, most of whom arrived there from other countries less than five years ago. While located in the middle of a metro area, the homogeneous community is essentially on an island. Isolated by lack of transportation, language, gang borders and fear of deportation, they are essentially cut off from city and county services. With parents having to travel to two, some times three, service jobs with erratic schedules, the children in this community are on their own—unsupervised, no positive role models and no positive alternative activities to steer them away from trouble.

What Is Your Target Population's
Point-Of-View?

That is, what is your Target Population's outlook and attitude toward others (such as teachers or health workers), institutions, their conditions, and their future? If their outlook is negative, how will their point-of-view hinder your Target Population trying to achieve the goals of your program?

Again, the hypothetical *For Example Arts After School Program* population: Because a majority of parents have formal schooling extending no further than 7th grade, they often see their children's schooling—and especially any extra curricula activities—as relatively unimportant. To them, school is a form of free daycare.

Are There Problems Of Perception?

"There are things known and there are things unknown, and in between are the doors of perception."

—William Blake

When possible, while researching and thinking about your Target Population—especially when conducting or reviewing surveys, focus groups and needs assessments—look beyond statistics for problems of perception: that is, how the Target Population fails to address or acknowledge their own problems and conditions. The reasons for these problems of perception are many and may include:

- Antiquated beliefs
- Cultural prejudices
- Fear and distrust of a system
- False assumptions and ignorance about an issue
- They are in denial

There is a sad-but-true example of how we included problems of perception in the Needs section of a federal GEAR UP grant. GEAR UP is a discretionary federal grant program designed to increase the number of low-income middle and high school students who are prepared to enter and succeed in post-secondary education.

In our example, results showed that more than 70% of middle and high school teachers polled believed that their students were not capable of successfully completing a four-year college or university. This was because students were not "ready and willing to work at their highest potential" because their parents didn't "actively encourage their children to prepare for college." The general consensus on the part of the teaching staff was that their students weren't "college material" so "why bother?" On the other hand, parents and guardians overwhelmingly reported that their children didn't understand the lessons or materials delivered by the teachers and that parent and students had great difficulty communicating with teachers and counselors. Because of these findings, the entire direction and focus of the grant changed—the teachers were as much a part of the problem as students and parents.

At the fictional *For Example Arts After School Program*, parents of student participants have a distrust of teachers and school staff, seeing them as part of a bewildering "system" that might report them at any time.

What Motivates Your Target Population?

What will motivate them to take ownership of a local problem? What will incite them to enthusiastically support a new idea? What will move your Target Population to act?

Let's take the at-risk students in the *For Example Arts After School Program*. They know that a positive academic experience can open many doors for them but, historically, classroom doors have been slammed in their face. We want to get them on campus, interacting with teachers, participating in the program and working toward a successful academic future.

So, what could motivate this group of at-risk students to step foot on campus? How about allowing them access to a computer lab so they could learn more about technology and improve their workplace skills? What about giving them school credit for some of their academic-based work they do in the program? What about a vocational program so they can work along side professionals and get real world experience? Maybe it's something as simple as at the end of each week, those with excellent attendance are treated to a movie night or given gift cards for a movie. The best thing to do is survey your target population. Let them decide. Who would know better what motivates them than them?

By determining your Target Population's motivators, you will not only tell the Reader/Scorer more about your population, you will also structure a more effective program design.

The "Aha!" Factor

One example of a specific "Aha!" factor for a specific Target Population can be found in a grant addressing the needs of a Target Population of 65+ year-old residents in a group of retirement homes. After a series of in-depth interviews, it was revealed that although this group lived in an affluent area that was not disproportionately victimized by serious crime, their level of anxiety was off the charts. This was attributed to their feeling of powerlessness: social isolation, physical disabilities that rendered them defenseless, their tendency to be less aware of and utilize services for victims of crime and the feeling that "no one cared" if they were victimized. This revelation was an "Aha!" for Reader/Scorers who assumed this age group's main concern would be health issues. So, by providing these seniors with fitness and self-defense classes their feeling of powerlessness was diminished (they were doing something about it) and because of this their mental and physical health improved as well. Aha!

How Is Your Target Population An Underdog?

An underdog was described as, "…one with the will and desire to change and give it their all despite the odds against them." A few examples of how the Target Population in the *For Example After School Program* could be positioned as an underdog in program design might include:

- A waiting list for already overcrowded programs, which shows they have the desire
- Families have agreed to take the initiative to raise funds that equal up to 25% of the grant program costs
- Families' willingness to pay a low-cost fee for services even though they might not be able to afford it

Remember the underdog theory here—*demonstrate* that your Target Population has the *will and desire* to improve their circumstances and beat the odds.

With the first two tasks complete (determining and defining the Target Population) it's time to move onto Task #3 where we answer the $64 million dollar question ... or is it 63 ...or 65 ...?

TASK #3
DECIDE ON THE NUMBER TO BE SERVED

Deciding on the number of the Target Population is a difficult strategic decision.

If you propose to provide services to *too many* of your Target Population, you run the risk of Reader/Scorers thinking you inflated the numbers to impress them. This is a strategy that can come back to bite you if your program has too few staff and not enough capacity to serve the inflated number.

If you decide to serve *too few* of your Target Population, then the Reader/Scorer might think that your program will not benefit enough people for the amount of money you are awarded—not enough bang for the buck.

For example, let's say you are in competition with a similar program in the same city and both your programs are asking for the same amount of money. The competing program proposes to serve 60 *more clients* per year than your program. Does the funding agency automatically support that other program that serves more clients than yours?

Not necessarily. Here's why.

Ten years ago, grants were funded based on "bang for the buck." In other words, the more clients that were provided services to for each dollar spent, the better the chances of receiving a grant award. At that time, grant applicants wanting to win money for their programs would project as high a number served as possible—inflating *the potential number served* in hopes of boosting the funding agency's bang for their buck. A few years after, lawmakers and budget makers determined that the money allocated to programs with these inflated numbers was being wasted —there was no accountability.

So now, funding agencies emphasize to grant applicants that the total number to be served shouldn't be highest on their priority list when deciding on the number of the Target Population. Instead of the greatest number, what they ask for is that your Planning Team: (1) select a manageable and measurable—but as large as possible—number of the Target Population, (2) document that the proposed program will work with this manageable size and then, (3) plan to gradually expand the program to a larger Target Population.

The key word: Manageable.

And because members of your Planning Team are experts about your target area and population, it is up to *you* to justify to the funding agency how you determine what defines a "manageable" number. To do that, your Planning Team needs to ask: How many clients can our staff efficiently and effectively manage with the money to be awarded? In addition, your Planning Team will also probably ask:

How Do We Know That The Number We Come Up With Is In The Ballpark?

Often, the RFP will define the number of Target Population to be served through *required staff-to-client ratios*. For example, in a child care grant, your state might mandate that there be no more than 12 students for each licensed caregiver. The RFP might also state that the projected budget range for each program is approximately $200,000. Calculating a preliminary budget shows that after required operating expenses you have funds enough to hire six licensed caregivers in a year. So multiply six caregivers times the student limit (12) and that equals 72 children per year.

Sometimes an RFP will provide parameters for the Target Population. In the case of a recently completed mentoring grant, a limit was put on awardees of $1,500 per year per child. So, if your strategy was to ask for $100,000, then you would have divided $100,000 by $1,500 to determine the number of clients served: approximately 65 students.

The bottom line? Don't think of bang for the buck. Think of *manageability*, *verifiable effectiveness*, and *strategic expansion* for the buck. Not as catchy a phrase but it will keep you in the ballpark.

To Duplicate or Unduplicate, That Is The Question

RFP/grant guidelines will often help you determine the number of Target Population to receive services in terms of being "duplicated" or "unduplicated."

Unduplicated means if, for example, you are designing a program for a health clinic, every time a person receives a service or referral it counts as one contact. So, while one client may make up to 15 visits per year for various reasons, s/he is counted as one unduplicated client. Unduplicated: Count the client once, not the number of contacts.

Duplicated means that you would count each client every time they come into the clinic or receive a service, regardless of the number of services they receive. So, if one client returns to the clinic 15 times in a year they are counted 15 times.

These are just two of many definitions. Do your homework. Find out exactly how the funding agency defines these terms.

Baseline Data

In some RFPs or grant guidelines you may read something like:

> Identify the baseline characteristics of the specific population to be served by the program..."

Baseline data is something quantifiable (tangible or measurable) that can be comparatively measured on a regular basis. Baseline data needs to be collected prior to the Target Population beginning the program. This initial (baseline) data is then used for comparison as participants progress through the program, when they leave, and/or down the line, sometimes years after they have left. This baseline data comparison is how you prove to the funding agency that what you're doing is working.

When you go on a diet, for example, your baseline data is what you weighed the day before you started your diet. Then, you determine how much weight you lose throughout each month by comparing your monthly weight to what you weighed in the beginning—your baseline data.

Letting The RFP Do The Work For You

One of the first steps in determining your Target Population should be to read the RFP very carefully (See Chapter 3-5).

The funding agency, in its application guidelines, often will dictate what age group, specific gender, ethnicities or other demographics they want you to target. They may also attach a few "risk factor" requirements (e.g., those who live with a family member who has a history of substance abuse, students who have been expelled more than twice in one school year, those who are uninsured, recent parolees, etc.).

For example, the RFP may contain a phrase like—

"... your primary goal should be to focus on children, particularly ages 2–5 who, historically, have not been emotionally and academically ready for kindergarten"

If that's the case, then a youth center designed to serve the entire target area's youth population (ages 6–19) is off the mark and would not get funded.

Often, RFPs will use a PRIMARY NEED INDICATOR. When the proposals are submitted, Reader/Scorers will go through and tally a preliminary ranking, putting those with the greatest percentage/number of that primary need indicator at the top of the list. Many times, in educational grants, this is the percentage of students a district has who qualify for free/reduced-cost lunches.

Or, rather than ranking the proposals, the funding agency may use a SINGLE NEED INDICATOR as a cutoff point to reduce the number of applicants. Using an educational grant as an example, a funding agency may require that only districts that have a minimum of 60% of their students eligible for free-/reduced-cost lunches will qualify. Then, those that fall short of that number are disqualified. Those over or above move forward for consideration.

Whatever the case, remember that just because a funding agency may use a primary indicator or a single need indicator as a cutoff, that DOES NOT mean it should be the ONLY need indicator your team uses in your program design.

TASK #4
DELINEATE YOUR TARGET AREA

When it comes to defining their target area, MOST applicants define their target area only in terms of geography. By doing so, they fail to "artfully sell the problem" by defining and delineating that area based on the obstacles and issues that target area presents to their Target Population. Your target area should be defined in four ways:

1. Clear, Definable Borders

Assume the Reader/Scorer is unfamiliar with your local area. Because of this, they won't see a picture of your target area unless you clearly delineate and describe it to them. This means you don't want to make a mistake made by MOST applicants of using a colloquial phrase like:

> "...what is known to those of us in the area as the "Southside.""

Why? Because there's nothing in the above phrase that offers the Reader/Scorer (who may live 3,000 miles from "Southside") a tangible description of the area.

However, if you continue on and *define* that area known as the "Southside" by its geographic borders, then it is good to use the pre-established name of an area. For example:

> Generic Elementary School is located in the
> target area known locally as "Southside," an
> eight-block, impoverished, gang-infested,
> historical district bordered by railroad tracks
> to the North, an interstate freeway to the
> west and an elementary school to the east.

Other options to help define the target area by borders
include:

- **Zip code/s:** These are sometimes the tool funding
  agencies use to define their target areas based on
  demographic research in collaboration with state
  and local agencies.
- **School Zones:** These are several blocks or a
  neighborhood surrounding a school.
- **Census Tracts:** Some applicants define an area by
  how the U.S. census defines the area through Census
  Tracts. Some of these areas are also known as a CDP
  (Census Designated Place), an unincorporated area
  recognized by the census bureau as a distinct area.
- **Residential Areas:** These could include a trailer
  park, a housing project, an affordable housing tract,
  student housing village, etc.
- **Political Districts:** These could include a school
  district, a portion of a city represented by a
  councilperson and/or a state assembly district.

- **Law Enforcement Jurisdictions:** This could include a Gun Free Zone or an area of a city that is part of a federal gang injunction.
- **Health Professional Shortage Area (HPSA):** This is a specific area deemed by the federal government as high-risk because of a shortage of qualified healthcare professionals.

Take a look at the following example (from a winning grant) of how we clearly defined the borders and also artfully sold the problem within the constraints of a 100-word limit:

> The geographic borders of the 1.3 square mile unincorporated area of Lennox (90304) are marked by three of the nation's most crowded freeways bordering the North, South and West. The Los Angeles World Airports Industrial complex is contiguous to the western border of the area. However, in a morbid reflection of the community's problems, Lennox is more clearly delineated by borders of more than 30 warring gangs— Asian gangs to the south, African-American gangs to the west and rival Latino gangs to the east.

2. Size of The Target Area

The size of the area in blocks, acres, or square miles, is also important to mention. Again, what Reader/Scorers look for here are clear, definable borders *within a manageable area.*

If your community is larger (i.e., unmanageable because of its sprawling size or high population density), target *a portion of the area, not the entire area.* Just make sure that portion of the area best presents a need. For example, assume the role of a Reader/Scorer for a moment and consider how these two target areas are presented:

Version One: The proposed program will serve 12% of Generic Town's population of 70,000+ who live at or below the poverty level.

Version Two: The proposed program will serve Generic Town's "Southside" area, an eight-block, impoverished, gang-infested, historic district where more than 90% of the 3,500+ families live at/below the poverty level.

Version One is too broad—an entire town.

Version Two narrows it down into a manageable area with a clear, definable border—and best presents a need.

If you operate within an impossibly large area (e.g., L.A. County is 4,000+ square miles with a population of more than 10 million people) make sure your target area is not so spread out that any alert Reader/Scorer will conclude that more staff time—and the program budget—will be spent on

http://vc.flo.org/ursa/staff_reqinq.sh

traveling and juggling logistics rather than actually providing direct services.

On the other hand, if you are designing a program for a rural or remote area with a large geographical expanse (I'm thinking of Inyo County here in California that is 10,000+ square miles with a population of less than 18,000), then use that remoteness as a selling point; that one of the main reasons that your Target Population has so many needs is that they are isolated from critically needed services.

3. Demographic/Socio-Economic Factors

"Artfully sell the problem" by describing the demographic and socio-economic make-up of your target area. The options here are limitless—until you remember that defining the target area should not be merely stating a grocery list of demographics but specific to the needs of, and obstacles faced by, your Target Population. Examples:

- **Population:** The area might be overcrowded with multiple families living in single-family dwellings. There could be a large community of homeless or transients. There might be a high percentage of single parent families with latchkey children.
- **Crime:** Look for target area crime rates and percentages that are significantly higher than local and/or state averages: number of gangs and gang-related crime, tagging, drug-related crime, domestic violence, etc.

- **Economic factors:** Again, look for rates and percentages significantly higher than local and/or state averages: percentage of population living at/below poverty level, unemployment rates, housing costs, number of renters vs. homeowners, etc.
- **Health factors:** This could include: a lack of human services available within and near the target area; a high percentage of uninsured residents; serious, unaddressed, health and mental health issues; or, a shortage of qualified healthcare professionals in your area.

4. Target Area – Other Risk Factors And Obstacles

As an example, let's say you are writing a school grant aimed at eliminating health risks in your students. You have used a School Zone (i.e., the school and 12 neighboring blocks) to define your area. You might then point out that the target area to be served is sandwiched in between two major freeways and directly under the flight path of the nation's second largest airport. These factors point to a number of air quality problems that would also need to be addressed.

Another way to further define this target area, by using risk factors, might be to indicate that this area is where a majority of juvenile crime (tagging, vandalism) is committed during after school hours, on Friday night and on the weekend.

Often, newspaper and magazine articles can help define and validate your target area in terms of risk factors. One target area I designed a program for was called "a gang murder hellhole." A County Sheriff spokesperson told a newspaper a target area was, "...home to the most impoverished, underserved and vulnerable youth population in the city." A state attorney general labeled another target area as a "culture of violence." All powerful statements provided by unbiased experts.

TASK # 5
DESCRIBE YOUR TARGET POPULATION

Any linguistic morphologists on your Planning Team? Didn't think so.

A linguistic morphologist is a highly specialized professional who scientifically studies word formation. But you need not be a linguistic morphologist to understand the importance of coming up with a few carefully chosen words to create a descriptor for your Target Population.

In simpler terms, remember the CB craze in the 1970s when everyone had a catchy, memorable name used to call and identify each other on the radio (did we actually listen to a song called *CB Savage?!*)? Think of a descriptor as a handle—good buddy. In other words, a few carefully chosen words that define your Target Population and are easy to remember. An effective descriptor:

- Describes and distinguishes your Target Population from others

- Constantly reminds the Reader/Scorer of your Target Population's needs
- Elicits strong emotional responses in the Reader/Scorer

Let's put on our linguistic morphologist hats (a beanie with a spinner on top?) and take a closer look at a too general descriptor—"elementary students"—to create a more effective descriptor.

While working on a series of mental health screenings for a program design, our Planning Team discovered that a large population of these "elementary students" were classified by counselors as "shy and withdrawn." These at-risk, K-3 students' lack of social skills and self-esteem put them at risk not only to become victims or perpetrators of violence, but also victims of substance abuse, gang involvement, suicide, teenage pregnancy, domestic violence and poor academic performance. Service providers and educators had typically overlooked this group of students because they had not yet acted out. In every aspect of the proposal, the descriptor we used was "shy and withdrawn K-3 students." It was more specific than elementary students, reminded the Reader/Scorer of our Target Population's needs and might even have produced a degree of empathy on the Reader/Scorer's behalf.

REVIEW QUESTIONS

Once you've applied the above elements to your own program design, review these questions to ensure you've covered all the bases.

1) Who (not what) is our program about?
2) Who is our specific Target Population?
3) What are at least four need indicators of our Target Population?
4) How are each of our need indicators supported by validated, relevant data?
5) How can we further define our Target Population by defining geographic boundaries?
6) What socio-economic conditions put our Target Population in a position where they need assistance?
7) How does the environment (where they live) provide obstacles and challenges to our Target Population?
8) How have environment and backstory shaped our Target Population's point-of-view?
9) What motivates our Target Population?
10) What need-related indicators can we use that will register on the "Aha!" meter of the Reader/Scorer?
11) What is our Target Population's descriptor?
12) How can we demonstrate that our Target Population is not just reactive, but proactive?

13) How does our definition of our Target Population align with the requirements of the RFP or the grant guidelines?

By using multiple factors to describe your Target Population, you've experienced, "…one of the joys of writing," as William Faulkner said, "when a character stands up and casts a shadow."

The need indicators used are pre-existing, constantly recurring conditions. However, they are not *the primary reason* your Planning Team should request support for your proposed program. The primary reason should be a sudden, severe, unexpected problem that has recently surfaced.

So, the plot thickens as we turn to the second "C" of *Jon's Almost World Famous Seven Cs!*

Chapter 2-4

Crisis In Movies
"A YUCKY MESS"

What happens when you blow a huge bubblegum bubble? It keeps getting bigger and bigger and more unwieldy until it eventually explodes into a yucky mess.

In the late 80s, Japanese animators adopted the phrase "Bubblegum Crisis" to describe their approach to developing plots in their cyberpunk-style animé. In animé plots, complications and conflict grow more intense and events get more and more out of control until, finally, all hell breaks loose and the bubble bursts.

The second "C" in *Jon's Almost World Famous Seven Cs!* is the main character's internal CRISIS. In movies, Crisis is an emotional/psychological bubble (i.e., issue) that grows and grows until, by the end of the story, either it destroys the character, or the character destroys it.

A therapist might call this Crisis an "emotional issue" that psychologically impedes a person from moving ahead with her/his life. When in Crisis, the person will stay hopelessly mired in this mental quicksand until s/he acknowledges that there is an issue, pinpoints its cause and therapeutically reconciles the issue.

In movies, what brings the character's long-festering Crisis to the surface are the events of the plot, other characters who create complications, and the main character's inner conflict. As the story progresses, these conflicts grow more intense and complicated. Tension builds. The character spirals more and more out of control until, finally, all hell breaks loose, the character faces his/her demons and explodes in a cathartic emotional/psychological purging.

A good example of this can be found in *Ordinary People,* the story of a family struggling to deal with the accidental death of one of their teenage sons. The surviving teenage son blames himself for his brother's drowning death that occurred a year earlier. This unresolved guilt (his Crisis) becomes too much to sublimate and begins to torment him in a series of nightmarish flashbacks. He becomes more disengaged from everything and everyone to the point of being suicidal.

A screenwriter uses Crisis as emotional baggage that hampers a main character from accomplishing what s/he wants in the story. This internal Crisis can be the result of the character's fears, traumatic events from the past, old emotional wounds, feelings of inadequacy, skeletons in the closet or having been traumatized. Whatever the reason, the character's Crisis has been sublimated and festering long before the plot begins.

Crisis And Emotional Depth

By having a character deal with her/his Crisis, it not only thickens the plot but brings complexity and emotional depth to the character.

One of the worst things a screenwriter can be accused of is writing "one note" characters; that is, characters who have only a single viewpoint, are only capable of a single emotion, or act in only one way. There are plenty of examples including the ditzy blonde, the bigoted southerner, and the soulless politician.

SCREENWRITING AXIOM #5

Any Good Story Is Told On More Than One Level

In movies, the plot may, on the surface, appear to be about one thing, such as the main character usually trying to achieve something material or trying to accomplish a physical challenge. But, beneath the surface—what the story is REALLY about—is that the hero must acknowledge, define, pinpoint the cause of, and reconcile her/his emotional or psychological Crisis before s/he can accomplish the Quest.

Take *Indiana Jones And The Last Crusade* for example. While the plot is about Indiana Jones teaming up with his father to find the Holy Grail before the Nazis, beneath the surface the movie is *really about* Indiana Jones finally stepping out from under the emotional/psychological shadow of his father. Not until Indy resolves his own Crisis (relating to his father) is he free to solve the problems of others.

On the surface, the movie *Rocky* is about his struggle to win the heavyweight championship. However, the movie is *really about* Rocky addressing his Crisis, which is lack of respect, by gaining respect from his neighborhood, his peers, his girl and, most importantly, himself.

SCREENWRITING AXIOM #6

The Main Character Should Be Unprepared To Deal With The Crisis

Maybe it's because the character is in denial. Or maybe it's because the events or characters that bring the Crisis to surface are unexpected. Whatever the reason, the character is often emotionally/psychologically unequipped and unprepared to deal with the Crisis. As a story unfolds, each scene becomes about the character acquiring and uncovering within her/himself the confidence, skills, tools, and power to overcome her/his Crisis.

Emotional Wallop

The emotional catharsis of a character confronting their Crisis is an aspect of screenwriting that novice screenwriters often choose to forego in lieu of a character confronting mindless, over-the-top, pyrotechnic plot devices such as big explosions, big battles and big contests.

However, ignoring this "C" has dire consequences on the emotional impact of a good story. And let's face it, veteran screenwriters—defined as those who have been writing and not making any money longer than novice screenwriters have been writing and not making any money—know that the bottom line of any good story is the emotional wallop it has on the main character.

Uncle Remus said, "You can't run away from trouble. There ain't no place that far." As with screenwriting, your program design needs to include a Crisis that your Target Population "can't run away from."

Chapter 2-5

Crisis In Program Design
A RECENT, UNEXPECTED PROBLEM

Now about the differences between a Crisis in a screenplay and Crisis in program design.

The movie Crisis has festered inside the main character long before the story starts. A movie Crisis is *internal* (psychological/emotional).

A program design's Crisis is *external*, impacts your Target Population, and should be a recent, unforeseen:

turn of events,

setback,

outbreak,

research finding,

threat from a group of people, or

an act of nature.

And, even if your program, agency or community does not have the resources, it needs to *immediately address* your Target Population's problem created by the Crisis.

That means, in your program design, your Planning Team *should not* think of Crisis in terms of problems such as a:

- Financial Crisis because of recent funding cuts to an agency
- Board of Directors' burnout because there are too many vacancies
- Overworked staff because there aren't enough qualified applicants to work at unfilled positions or
- Recently lost clients due to competition from another agency

These problems, while all serious and worthy, are about your program and staff—*not your Target Population.*

Don't Confuse Need Indicators With Crisis

Need indicators (discussed in Chapter 2–3) are *chronic*: that is, pre-existing conditions that have persisted for a long time and are constantly recurring.

A program design Crisis is acute: that is, a sudden, severe, intense problem facing your Target Population that springs up unexpectedly.

"Artfully Selling" The Crisis

Considering the immediacy and unexpectedness of this Crisis, it is not a negative to admit to the funding agency that there is a shortcoming in your program services and that, without their support, you do not have the resources to address the Crisis. Funding agencies actually support grant applicants who are honest about their unexpected crises—as long as they are articulated well, supported by data, and there's a solid plan to fix them within a reasonable amount of time.

In terms of "artfully selling the problem", your Planning Team should consider your Crisis a positive. Without this Crisis, all your team will be requesting is funds for current operations or duplicative services, something MOST grant writers do—and remember, MOST grant writers don't win.

The Crisis In Question

Answering the questions below is the most effective way for your Planning Team to define and describe your local Crisis.

To help with your answers, I'm going to offer examples using a fictitious universal preschool program whose lead agency is a fictional school district. Let's say this program is in the second year of a four-year grant. We'll call the program: *The Camp Wannabe Preschool Program.*

Crisis Question #1: What is the immediate Crisis that negatively impacts our Target Population?

Keep your answer simple. Limit it to *one Crisis* that can be described in a single, short, succinct sentence. You'll be asked to further define and describe the Crisis in the questions that follow.

Make sure that your Crisis is a *recent, unexpected* problem—within the last year—that did not previously exist when you originated your program.

Your proposed grant-related Crisis cannot be something outside the scope and responsibility of your initial grant request or your program/agency's area of expertise. For example, if your senior nutrition program's mission is to provide meals to isolated, low-income seniors who suddenly have an alarmingly high rate of cataracts—those two problems (hunger and vision) aren't related.

Here are more examples of crises that I've used in program designs:

- A local natural disaster such as Hurricane Katrina
- A local outbreak of Hepatitis C
- The closing of a Healthy Start clinic, a Target Population's only local source of low-/no-cost immunizations
- An unexpected rise in community college tuition rates at a local college attended by a low-income target population
- A partner who promised a matching fund unexpectedly withdrew their promised services that were vital to the target population
- Asbestos found in offices and meeting rooms where the target population received services
- A new education test or assessment results showed students within the target population were underperforming at a rate higher than local or state averages

For the Wannabe Preschool example I'll use the last item from the list above.

- In test results released for the first time within the last month, it was revealed that the level of kindergarten readiness of Camp Wannabe four-year olds lags behind more affluent communities in the state by as much as 18 months.

Crisis Question #2: **What empirical proof do we have that this Crisis actually exists?**

Empirical means observable, measurable.

The focus here is on *measuring* your Target Population's stated Crisis—and the stated Crisis only.

Just as you must demonstrate need indicators, you must also prove every claim and assertion of a Crisis with reliable, timely, empirical data. A grant-related Crisis should not be based on a hunch, theory, or your staff merely getting a sense that trouble is brewing.

So for now, and to keep it simple, identify just one key measurement tool that proves your Crisis exists.

MEASUREMENT is the key word here.

Let's continue with the Wannabe example:

- These findings are based on the school district's newly implemented "Kindergarten

Readiness Test," recognized as the most accurate assessment of readiness by the state department that funds the program.

Crisis Question #3: **What are the main causes of our Crisis?**

Your Crisis is the *effect.* Now it's time to determine the *causes* of the Crisis. Members of your Planning Team should be the experts here.

To better focus your answers, first restate the problem as is illustrated in the Wannabe example below:

- The three main reasons that Wannabe four-year olds scored lower on the Kindergarten Readiness Test than more affluent communities in the state are:
  - *Language barriers:* In the past two years, the number of Wannabe students who are English Learners (ELs) has increased from 30% to 85% (statewide, the average is 18%). The test is administered in English only.
  - *Limited bilingual staff:* Although 85% of the students are Limited English Proficient, less than 20% of staff are bilingual.
  - *Budget cuts:* Recent budget cutbacks and a hiring freeze have led to the elimination of the district's bilingual Early Reader

Resources Specialist who helped these EL
students and who conducted EL-related
professional development for staff.

Crisis Question #4: Why did our Crisis *recently* occur?
Recent = within the past year.

If your Crisis is not a recent occurrence, then any astute
Reader/Scorer will wonder why your Planning Team never
bothered to address the problem before. In their mind, you
might as well just write, "Dear Reader/Scorer: Please give
us money because we didn't think of these things when we
should have."

So, answering this question about your Crisis being a
recent occurrence will ensure that your Planning Team
doesn't request funds for current operations or duplicative
services that address pre-existing conditions.

Here's an answer to why the Wannabe Crisis *recently*
occurred:

- This lag in kindergarten readiness levels has gone
  unaddressed until now for two main reasons:
  1. The new Kindergarten Readiness test
     was administered by the state for the
     first time last spring, two months ago.
     Results were not released to schools until
     last month. Prior to then, there was no
     standardized test.

2. An unexpected drop in district enrollment resulted in a district hiring freeze that has been in effect for the past year. Because of this, the repercussions of not having a bilingual Early Reader Resource Specialist are just now surfacing.

Crisis Question #5: How is our Target Population's Crisis local and unique?

While it's okay and typical for your Target Population to suffer from the same Crisis as other populations around the country, it's your Planning Team's job to take those national trends to another level—in this case, your local target area. Remember to use comparative statistics.

- The number of Wannabe four-year olds who are 18 months behind where they should be in their cognitive development is three times greater than neighboring districts in the area and seven times greater than the state average.
- The Wannabe student EL rate (85%) is the highest of any preschool in the county.
- The Wannabe Preschool program is the only formal, standards-based, preschool program of its kind in the target area; others only offer day care and informal, non-standards based literacy instruction.

- Unlike more affluent parents in neighboring communities, Wannabe parents won't and can't travel outside the area for additional services because of safety, transportation and financial issues.

- Wannabe parents' work schedules are atypical and unpredictable; most work two service-orientated jobs with erratic schedules that don't coincide with school schedules.

Crisis Question #6: If this Crisis is not immediately and adequately addressed, what are the repercussions?

Three points to consider as you establish what's at stake.

First, *the local ripple effect.* How does it effect and impact other aspects of your Target Population's lives? Their families? The district? The community? The local political system?

Second, what will be the *immediate repercussions* if this Crisis is not addressed?

Third, what are the *long-term repercussions* if this Crisis is not addressed?

1) One immediate repercussion is that if Camp Wannabe scores are not improved, state funding will cease and the community will lose its only, formalized state standards-based preschool program.

2) Another immediate repercussion is that low kindergarten readiness levels drain district resources through the inordinate cost of additional reading intervention programs and specialists.

3) In the long term, for every $1 invested in early child care/preschool programs, over $7 is saved in later payments made through health, social service, justice and educational agencies.

4) Wannabe students who do not attend preschool fall behind in kindergarten and never catch up academically. Based on one local university study, 65% of Wannabe students who did not participate in preschool did not complete high school, compared to only 8% of their kindergarten-ready peers.

✛ ✛ ✛

Remember, this "C" – Crisis – is about *defining and describing* the repercussions of the Crisis. It is not about solving the Crisis. How you intend to solve the Crisis begins with the third "C" of *Jon's Almost World Famous Seven Cs!*

Chapter 2-6

The Movie Cuest
THAT'S RIGHT, CUEST WITH A "C"

What do you want me to do, change them to *Jon's Almost World Famous Six and a Q!?* Doesn't have quite the same ring does it? CUEST with a "C"—it's the best I could do. Just go with it.

Que- uh, Cuest in the movies refers to what or who the *main character* is:

pursuing,

trying to solve,

searching for, or

trying to achieve.

That's it—it's that simple.

Screenwriters often refer to the main character's Cuest as the "machine that drives the story." That is, the Cuest gives the main character a purpose, keeps the story moving to a conclusion and motivates the audience to watch the story until the end to see if the Cuest is achieved.

Once main characters have a Cuest, or a mission, they become much more focused, purposeful and organized—all in order to achieve their final goal.

The Cuest has another benefit to the screenwriter. Once a Cuest is firmly embedded into the story as the main character's primary motivator, the screenwriting process becomes more focused, purposeful and organized. That's because every line of dialogue, every scene, every sequence and every act break becomes about the character trying to overcome obstacles and achieve the Cuest.

Screenwriting Axiom #7

The Character's Cuest Should Be Tangible, Not Abstract

Most good movie Cuests are tangible, as in physical or perceptible. When characters achieve their Cuest they can hold it, hear it, touch it, taste it, see it or stand on it. A Cuest may be to: cross the finish line first, hold up the trophy, marry the dream girl, find a buried treasure, or track down the murderer. This tangibility factor is especially critical in movies because movies are a visual medium—stories told in pictures. This means the audience needs to be able to *see* if the Cuest has been accomplished.

An abstract Cuest in a movie is generally a no-no. For example, a novice screenwriter may come up with an abstract Cuest such as:

> "It's about a young woman's search to find out who she really is in these confusing, troubled times."

Too abstract.

Sure, the character finding herself is what the movie may really be about beneath the surface—in other words, the message. But as movie mogul Sam Goldwyn once said to a screenwriter, "If you want to send a message use Western Union."

Back to the abstract novice. If, for example, her protagonist runs away overseas to find her fugitive, ex-Mafioso father, then finding the father becomes a *tangible* Cuest.

Screenwriting Axiom #8

There Should Only Be One Main Cuest

There may be several other goals the main character is trying to achieve in the story. There may be a multitude of obstacles that the main character needs to overcome. But there should be only one main *Overarching Cuest* that drives the character and story forward. This is so the main character—and all those on his or her side—are heading in the same direction, fighting the same crusade.

Speaking of crusade, let's again use the movie *Indiana Jones And The Last Crusade* as an example. Indy's Overarching Cuest isn't to find the Holy Grail—*and* find his father— *and* to save the girl—*and* to avenge the bad guy—*and* to rescue his friend from the museum—*and* to defeat the Nazis—*and* to reconcile with his father— *and* to preserve other holy relics.

Indy's single *Overarching Cuest* is to find the Holy Grail.

It's that simple.

An Overarching Cuest makes the main character pursuing it become much more focused, purposeful and organized—all in order to achieve their final goal.

Now let's read how creating an Overarching Cuest for your Target Population will make your Planning Team's program design more focused, purposeful and organized.

Chapter 2-7

The Cuest Of Your Program Design
A SIMPLE, SINGLE ENDPOINT

Just as screenplays have one Overarching Cuest, your program design should have one Overarching Cuest.

For program design, however, change "Overarching Cuest" to the phrase "Overarching Goal."

An Overarching Goal gives your program design:

Focus

Purpose

Organization

If, at the end of your grant period, your program has empowered your Target Population to achieve their Overarching Goal, you have succeeded.

However, don't confuse your program design's Overarching Goal with:

- Your program's or agency's existing mission statement, or

- The details about how you intend to solve your Target Population's stated problems

Here's The Good Part

You've already done most of the work. Why? Because, the first two steps of this program design process are to: (1) define your Target Population, and (2) determine their single, primary Crisis.

With those first few steps complete, the Overarching Goal of your program design is about addressing your Target Population's Crisis.

Formulating And Phrasing

If how we write is how we think, then the process of formulating, simplifying, then phrasing a simple, singular Overarching Goal will help give your program design a clear, focused purpose as well.

Before you formulate and phrase your Overarching Goal, let's look at an example. First, the Crisis we came up with for our Camp Wannabe preschoolers:

- In test results released for the first time within the last month, it was revealed that the level of kindergarten readiness of Camp Wannabe four-year olds lags behind more affluent, communities in the state by as much as 18 months.

Can you come up with the simple, singular Overarching Goal of the Camp Wannabe program design?

The answer is simple because the Overarching Goal of your program design is about addressing your Target Population's Crisis.

- Improve the kindergarten-readiness level of Camp Wannabe students.

That's it: their simple, singular Overarching Goal.

The Five Point Overarching Goal Inspection

To help formulate and phrase your program's Overarching Goal, have your Planning Team answer the following:

1. Does Our Overarching Goal Begin With An Action/Improvement Verb?

Your Overarching Goal should be stated in terms of how your Planning Team envisions the Target Population changing or transforming or improving. So, begin your Overarching Goal with an active verb like "increase," "improve," "reduce" or "expand." Any active verb that connotes improvement or positive change will work.

➡ In the Wannabe example, the Overarching Goal starts with the verb "Improve."

2. Does Our Overarching Goal Avoid the "A-Word"?

Avoid using "And," a conjunctive phrase that ties together two separate thoughts or ideas.

"And" tends to complicate, compound and confuse.

Your Overarching Goal should be *one simple, singular task*, not a shopping list of various tasks. Your Overarching Goal should never leave a Reader/Scorer saying to him or herself "...so which is it?"

➡ In the Wannabe example, the simple, singular Overarching Goal does not contain the "A–Word."

3. Does Our Overarching Goal Avoid Mentioning Solutions?

Mention nothing about solving the problems or steps to addressing the Overarching Goal. The solving part of your program design will come later. The Overarching Goal is simply what you want your program to achieve for your Target Population.

➡ In the Wannabe example, there is no discussion of how they intend to improve scores, the new staff training needed, how parents will become involved or ways of better preparing students for the test.

4. Is Our Overarching Goal Twenty Words Or Less?

Keep it short and sweet.

Don't discuss it, state it.

Save details and explanations for the proposal narrative. Remember, the more specific the Crisis, the more succinct your Overarching Goal will be.

➥ The Wannabe example is 10 words.

5. Is Our Overarching Goal Measurable?

An Overarching Goal should be something tangible—measurable—and not esoteric or attitudinal such as "To raise awareness..." or "Come to a better appreciation of..." "...uplift the spirits of..." You should be able to *prove* that the Overarching Goal has been attained through quantifiable data (we'll discuss this later).

➥ At Camp Wannabe, kindergarten readiness is measured by a standardized state test.

✢ ✢ ✢

Coming up with an Overarching Goal for your program design is relatively easy. Achieving the Overarching Goal is often a challenging process where time is of the essence—or it should be, so read on.

Chapter 2-8

The Ticking Clock In Movies
MOVIES MUST KEEP MOVING

If audiences are not on the edge of their seat, then storytellers are on the edge of failure.

We've all had those moments in a movie theater where the story just seems to run out of gas. We fidget, start chewing on the kernels at the bottom of the popcorn bag, look at our watch and wish we had some sort of fast forward device on the armrest.

If this occurs with a majority of viewers at a sneak preview where the nervous filmmakers are in the back row studying audience reactions to the first rough cuts of their movies, they know they are doomed.

That is why I've often thought that film school instructors should teach their student storytellers to think of the projector showing the stories they write as running on the collective will of the audience.

Instead of chairs, the audience would pedal stationary bikes that power the projector in the booth. If the story is told at the proper pace, the audience would energetically pedal away, providing full power to the projector. If the movie slowed and bored, the audience's attention would wane, the pedaling would slow and the projector would dim. If the audience cared less about what happened, they would stop pedaling and the projector would come to a dead stop.

So what is a trick that screenwriters use to keep the audience pedaling—or, I should say, the story moving?

A Ticking Clock

And, no, the one on the mantel over the hero's shoulder in the second scene doesn't count.

This is a story clock—embedded in the structure and directly tied to the Cuest. In other words, the main character of the story must complete their Cuest in a certain period of time.

In fact, Clock is so essential to the storytelling process that it often becomes part of the title (and a movie's marketing campaign): *High Noon, 48 Hours, 24, 25th Hour, Three Days of the Condor, Around The World In Eighty Days, 3:10 to Yuma, Countdown to D-Day,* etc.

A Clock provides the story with an overriding sense of urgency, a do or die deadline. A clock provides the viewer with reason to wonder and worry if, and how, the main character is going to achieve the Cuest.

With a Clock, a good screen story becomes more than the hero's race against another character to achieve the Cuest—it also becomes a race against time.

Types Of Story Clocks In Movies

The deadline. With this type of story clock, the Cuest needs to be achieved before an exact time. Example: In *High Noon*, a retiring lawman is about to leave town in the morning with his new bride when he learns that a gunslinger he sent to prison has been released and is arriving on the noon train to seek revenge.

The Running Clock. This type of story is told in real time. Example: *Nick of Time* is about a middle-class CPA whose daughter is kidnapped. He is given a gun and a picture of a person, and told that if he hasn't killed that person in one hour and fifteen minutes, his daughter will be killed. We then follow him continuously for the next 75 minutes.

An impending event. This one does not revolve around a specific time, but instead a looming or impending event such as the death of a character who is just barely hanging on, the crossing of two characters' paths or a natural disaster. For example, the tagline on the poster for the movie *Asteroid* features the clock of an impending event: "Heaven and Earth are about to collide."

Screenwriting Axiom #9:

A Story Clock Should Pass The "Or Else..." Test

The word deadline originated in Civil War prison camps when there were few formal prisons with walls. Instead, prisoners would be herded into an open space and a line drawn around them as a border. If any prisoner crossed that line, the consequence was that the prison guards shot them dead.

When a Clock is inserted into a story, a do-or-die deadline also needs to be inserted—a time when the Cuest must be accomplished.

Screenwriters give the deadline consequence by making sure that it is as close to the true meaning of the word deadline as possible. Because if there's not a lot at stake for the main character to achieve the Cuest by the deadline then there's no sense of urgency in the story.

The way to verify that? Give a story Clock the "Or else..." test. Here's an example:

Let's say I was telling you a story about...

> ...a woman trying to get to a safe deposit box
> in her bank before the doors close at 4 p.m. It
> is absolutely essential that she get
> to the bank before 4 p.m...

Or else...?

> ...or else, uh, she has to show up the next
> morning when the bank opens at 9 a.m.

Ho-hum.

There's no real urgency—nothing's really at stake—nothing's hanging in the balance. No sense of threat, no jeopardy, no do or die.

Try this new and improved version where we raise the stakes by giving the clock an "or else:"

> This is a story about a woman trying to get to a safe deposit box in her bank before the doors close at 4 p.m...

Or else...?

> ...or else the kidnappers holding her son will kill him.

Much better, right?

A bit of a cliché perhaps, but that's not the point. The point is that there's something meaningful at stake now. By inserting a Clock with a do-or-die consequence into the story—in other words, a Clock that passes the "Or else" test —a necessary sense of urgency is added.

Screenwriting Axiom #10:

The Shorter The Window Of Opportunity, The Better The Clock

Just as achieving the Cuest should seem nearly impossible for the main character, so too should her/his chances of achieving the Cuest within the deadline.

The more that window of time is shortened in the story—that is, the less time the hero has to accomplish the

Cuest before the "or else" happens—the greater the odds, the greater the urgency and the greater impact the story has on the audience.

For example, a story may be about someone who has to drive across country from L.A. to Boston to prevent the wedding of her best friend. And she has only…six months to get there.

Six months?

Any doubt she'll make it? No.

Any sense of urgency? No.

Any real pressure put on the character because of the six-month deadline? No real pressure. In fact, the character would only have to drive 13 miles a day to make it.

Let's shrink the clock more. Let's say…40 hours. That's one hour for every 75 miles. Again doable—but only if the character doesn't stop to eat, sleep, drink or bathe and commits almost every moving violation one can in a vehicle. And then, she'll only get there if absolutely nothing goes wrong. No way she can make it, we think…or is there?

The "or is there?" is what keeps the audience watching.

The Tick-Tock Hall of Fame?

If there was a "Story Clock Hall Of Fame" somewhere, this example would be enshrined there. It's *D.O.A.*, the classic B-movie starring Edmond O'Brien. *D.O.A.* is a thriller about a detective who has been poisoned and must find his own murderer and the antidote before the poison kills him in less than a week.

Now THAT's a ticking clock with consequence.

✛   ✛   ✛

A do-or-die deadline—a short window of opportunity—the "or else…" factor—let's take a look at how a "ticking clock" can add a sense of urgency to your program design.

Chapter 2-9

Clock In Program Design
"WHY NOW AND NOT LATER?"

Anyone who promotes a follow-these-steps-and-answer-the-questions-this-way-and-we-guarantee-you-will-win-fistfuls-of-grant-money is (as the old joke goes), "either lying or trying to sell you something."

The reality is that there are more excellent grants than there are grant dollars to fund them. This is especially frustrating for Reader/Scorers when they have before them more well-crafted, deserving program designs than they do remaining funding slots and the Grant Gods can only choose a few from all the equally meritorious applicants.

Often this decision comes down to the Reader/Scorer asking one single burning question about each finalist's program design:

"Why does this applicant's program need funding *now* and not later?"

It is often the applicant who has the *most urgent deadline* and most clearly articulates the repercussions of the "or else" factor linked to that deadline that wins the remaining award money.

Here are five questions to help your Planning Team determine and define a "ticking clock" that will ensure your program design will be more competitive and fundable.

As we look at each question, we'll create an example with a little help from our friends from Camp Wannabe Preschool. First, let's restate Camp Wannabe's Overarching Goal:

> **To improve the kindergarten readiness level of Camp Wannabe students.**

Question #1:
Do We Have A "Now, Not Later" Sense Of Urgency?

Just as the clock in screen stories is tied into the (Overarching) Cuest, your program design's clock should be tied into your program design's Overarching Goal.

A screenwriter's aim is to shrink the window of time and make it difficult—seemingly impossible—for the main character to achieve his/her Cuest within that time period.

In your program design, make the repercussion immediate—as close as possible to the time of the deadline.

First, here is an example of a *not-so-immedi*ate deadline:

> ...if the Camp Wannabe 3–4 year olds do not receive the requested support before the upcoming school year, then these students will most likely not receive a college degree.

While it is true that those never attending preschool are less likely to end up in college than those who do, that long-term repercussion is *more than 15 years down the road.*

In program design, the deadline your Planning Team chooses should answer the "Why now, not later?" question:

> Camp Wannabe Preschool Program funding renewal depends on whether test scores improve, as reviewed by the state in 20 months.

Question #2:
What Is The "Or Else" Factor Of Our Clock?

If the Overarching Goal of your program design is not achieved by a certain period of time what will happen? What will be the repercussion? I'm not suggesting it literally has to be "do or die"—as it often is in the world of movie make believe. But the repercussion should be something serious: loss of services, a health risk, financial hardship, etc.

What is the "Or Else" factor of Camp Wannabe's clock of a state review in 20 months?

> The bottom line: No improvement in state
> test scores = no further funding.

Question #3:
How Does The Clock And Or Else Factor Relate To Our Target Population?

Make sure that the repercussions of not meeting your deadline are related directly to your Target Population and not your program or agency.

> Camp Wannabe is the only preschool program
> in the impoverished area. Without funding,
> needy preschoolers in the target area would
> be left with no program to attend.

Question #4:
Is Our Clock Realistic?

Be realistic and consider the timetable of the funding agency. Don't make a case for needing grant funds within the next three weeks when the agency clearly states, for example, that it will take them at least seven months to consider applications, make their decision, conduct site visits, and then announce and award the grants.

As another example, you wouldn't request support to design, gain approval, build, equip and staff a charter high school by the time the new school year begins in four months. Because knowing that goal is an impossibility, a Reader/Scorer would not seriously consider you or your request.

Let's see if Camp Wannabe's Clock is realistic:

> Twenty months isn't a lot of time to roll out a program that would improve children's skills, but it is doable. Improvements could occur with the right staff, resources and stakeholder support—if we get started now and not later.

Back to the Reader/Scorer

Picture a Reader/Scorer reviewing three excellent preschool program designs. She can only choose one for funding. She opens the Camp Wannabe grant and reads:

> The Camp Wannabe program's overarching goal is to improve graduates' kindergarten readiness scores, which lag behind similar age groups in more affluent communities by as much as 18 months. The Camp Wannabe Preschool Program will be eligible for funding renewal when it is reviewed by the state in 20 months. A mandatory state requirement is

> a statistically significant increase in Wannabe
> graduates' kindergarten readiness scores. If
> no improvement in test scores occurs, then
> Camp Wannabe will become permanently
> ineligible for additional state funds and be
> forced to shut down, leaving the impoverished
> area with no preschool program.

Would Camp Wannabe's program design be funded with the highly defined clock above? I would never presume to predict what the Grant Gods would or wouldn't ultimately fund. There are just too many variables.

But, I do guarantee that the Camp Wannabe proposal would be *seriously considered* for funding. Why? Their ticking Clock compellingly answers the question asked by the Reader/Scorer that is often the difference between a program design awarded funding or ending up like MOST program designs:

"Why now and not later?"

Clocking In With Other Examples

Maybe your program or agency has an offer of support and you have three months to raise matching funds or the offer will be withdrawn—then you've got a great clock.

If current funding of your program by another grant sunsets in one year and you are seeking additional resources from another grant to continue a one-of-a-kind program that is essential to the community, that's urgency.

In the last few years, with the emphasis on the high school exit exam, many winning grants have pitched an accelerated academic assistance program for high school students in time for them to pass the test and graduate by their senior year. The end-of-year test was the deadline.

With the *No Child Left Behind* cloud hanging over public education, underperforming schools have a certain period of time to improve test scores. If not, they have to relinquish control to state authorities.

Let's try health care. For whatever reason, an area has a sudden population explosion of young mothers with infants ages three months to one year. A costly immunization is required before they turn two years old. That means money has to be found somewhere to offer free vaccines. The deadline? If, by the time this group reaches age two they aren't vaccinated, they run a risk of acquiring the debilitating virus. With a large percentage of the Target Population being one year olds, that means the process would have to be up and running within 12 months.

The urgency? 12 months.

The repercussion? The debilitating effects of the virus and more costly health care costs down the road.

✛ ✛ ✛

With the Character, Crisis, Cuest and Clock, it seems as though all is in place. But there are obstacles in the road to attaining the Cuest. With the fifth "C" of *Jon's Almost World Famous Seven Cs!*, you'll learn how to "artfully sell" those negative obstacles by transforming them into a positive element of your program design.

Chapter 2-10

Conflict in Movies
NO CONFLICT = NO STORY

America's most prolific playwright, Neil Simon, once shared his trick for telling a good story: put opposites in the room and let them have at each other.

Let's hope that doesn't describe your Planning Team at this point in the process.

What it does describe is the oxygen of any good story and the fifth of *Jon's Almost World Famous Seven Cs!*:

CONFLICT.

Without Conflict, a story asphyxiates.

Often, in the planning and plotting stages of creating a story, writers find themselves like a fly in a spider's web—hopelessly entangled in the complexities of their story logic. The more they struggle to wrestle free, the more stuck they become.

To unstick them, I have them reduce their story to one simple sentence by filling in the blanks of the following:

"My story is about [*the main character*] trying to achieve [*the Cuest*] and [*who and what*] is preventing her/him from achieving it."

Whittling a complex, multi-character story down to a sentence is not as easy as it sounds. But when the frustrated writer finally does manage to trim away the fat and get to the meat of the story—the weakness is exposed.

There's no meat.

And, at the risk of butchering this meat metaphor even more, the meat of a story is the conflict: the "who and what" preventing the character from achieving her/his Cuest.

Any screenwriter worth their weight in caffeinated peppermints knows it's their job to stack the odds against the main character every step of the way, at every turn. And just when all the Conflict and obstacles seem insurmountable to the main character—the writer's job is to invent a new way to crank up the Conflict another notch.

And we're talking Conflict in EVERY scene of a movie, not just at the end or at key points—every scene—every step of the plot. Conflict in storytelling comes in all shapes and sizes but we're going to categorize it into three types.

Physical Obstacles And Barriers

Think of physical Conflict as the "what" that stands in the way of the character achieving her/his Cuest.

In terms of natural elements this could be obstacles such as a raging river, a mysterious forest, the surface of an unexplored

planet or the no-oxygen effects of climbing the highest peak. A man-made barrier could be a prison wall, a border between two nations, a road potted with land mines or a disabled spacecraft lost in space somewhere. A third type of physical Conflict are physical traits that may impede a character. This could include having to be in a wheelchair, physical appearance, an injury or wound, physical weakness or blindness.

External Conflict

This is the "who" standing in the way.

When you think of external Conflict think of Conflict personified—meaning, an individual or group standing in the character's way of achieving the Cuest—whether they mean to or not.

First, let's look at external Conflict personified by an individual. The most recognizable of these characters is the antagonist—the primary character standing in the way of the protagonist trying to achieve her/his Cuest.

Can you say Darth Vader? Wicked Witch of the West? Hannibal Lecter? Gollum?

The more formidable the antagonist, the more challenge it is for the main character. And the greater the challenge and the Conflict the main character must rise above, the better it defines the character and the more the audience roots for the character.

The second type of Conflict comes from a *group of* people. Remember mores (pronounced more-ays) from sociology class?

Mores are a traditional custom or belief practiced by a group of people or a society. Here's an example of Mores:

> A young girl from a conservative small town falls in love with a professional wrestler. Love conquers all—or so she thinks until she finds herself pitted against the conservative traditions of her family, the townspeople and church members who all want to run them out of town.

Now *that's* amores! (Sorry Dino.)

Internal Conflict

Step inside your own head for a moment (do you hear an echo?) and think of Conflicts in your own life—that is, what is it *about you* that is preventing you from achieving the personal goals you want to achieve? No doubt, the most challenging, complex and formidable barriers stopping you from achieving your own personal Cuest are those created by you.

That is true for screen characters created on the page as well. Remember the chapter on "Crisis?" The internal Crisis deals with deep-seeded, unaddressed emotional and psychological obstacles and issues. We're talking fears, paranoia, low self-esteem, complexes, too much self-esteem, schizophrenia or various life scripts the character is acting out.

These are the internal Conflict.

The Simple Equation

The most important thing to remember about this fifth "C" of *Jon's Almost World Famous Seven Cs!* is a simple equation:

No Conflict = no story.

This simple equation is also important to your program design. How important? Here's a new equation that might get your attention:

No Conflict in your program design = no grant money.

Chapter 2-11

Conflict in Program Design
NO CONFLICT = NO GRANT MONEY

Conflict in program design can be defined as the WHO and the WHAT standing in the way of your Target Population achieving their Overarching Goal.

For those of you who have defined your Target Population, their Crisis and their Overarching Goal, then defining your Target Population's Conflict takes four steps:

> *Step One:* **Brainstorming**
> *Step Two:* **Weeding Out**
> *Step Three:* **Grouping and Prioritizing**
> *Step Four:* **Summarizing**

A Few Reminders About Conflict

Before I start with the first part of this step-by-step process, a few reminders about conflict:

- **Focus:** Remember how specific we were in getting the wording right about your Target Population's

Overarching Goal? Keep that same sense of focus
as you detail your Target Population's conflicts. To
do that, make sure that each element of Conflict is
directly related to the Overarching Goal. Or, as stated
in the Bill Of Writes, "...the main thing is to keep the
main thing the main thing."

- **Only identify problems, complications and
  obstacles:** As tempted as you might be, don't invent
  solutions or fixes at this point, even though they're
  seemingly jumping off the page and wanting to type
  themselves. Solutions will be addressed in subsequent
  chapters.

- **Go beyond the usual suspects:** As you identify areas
  of conflict, try to think beyond what you've come up
  with in past grants and what other applicants are sure
  to think of. If you always do what you've always done,
  you'll always get the same results.

- **Think local:** Which conflicts are unique to your
  target area and Target Population (i.e., those that
  will help you stand out from other applicants)? Sure,
  programs like yours across the nation share some of
  the same obstacles, sources of conflict and challenges.
  But it's up to your Planning Team to point out why
  your problems may be more serious than other
  programs and which are unique to your local area.

STEP ONE: BRAINSTORMING

There are three ways to come up with a Target Population's Conflict for your specific program design. Use any one or any combination of three. What works best for your Planning Team is what matters most at this stage. There are no right answers here. Final choices will vary depending on the type of grant you're writing, your target area and Target Population.

In a brainstorming session without censoring or editing each other—or turning it into a blamestorming session—list all the various forms of conflict your Planning Team can think of. No matter how far-fetched you or any member of your Planning Team may think an idea is, anything goes. Remember, what you may harbor as a silly idea may be just that, but saying it aloud may either see it resoundingly accepted by the others or may spur another member of the Planning Team to think of a slightly better variation. So, at this point, just make the list of all possibilities. Don't worry about which may be right or wrong or how long your list should be.

Option One:
The Three Categories

The first option is to use the three categories that many screenwriters use when they come up with conflict for their main character:

- **Physical conflict:** What is it about your target area and/or contiguous areas, that present obstacles for your

Target Population? Some examples: long distances from available resources, environmental risk factors, limited public transportation, safety-related factors, crime rates, proximity to undesirable locations, technology-related challenges, population density, high housing costs, or lack of law enforcement in the area. What about your Target Population's physical condition, such as health factors (e.g., obesity, teen pregnancy rates) or age? Here are examples of physical conflict I've used in recent grant proposals:

- A lack of facilities (e.g., office space, private meeting areas, play areas, storage)
- Transportation obstacles (parking, lack of drop-off areas, costs, etc.)
- High crime rates in an area
- ADA accessibility factors
- A lack of safety measures (e.g., lighting, fences, security cameras, locks)
- Proximity to undesirable locations (a race track, liquor store, high crime area, airport, busy streets)
- Lack of access to technology or lack of technology equipment
- Environmental risk factors (poor drinking water, poor air quality, environmental noise)
- Population density (overcrowded housing, housing shortages)
- The relatively high cost of living in the area

- **External conflict:** This is conflict personified—the WHO (individuals and groups) that may be in the way of your Target Population achieving their Overarching Goal. In past grants I've worked on, these have included:
  - Racial conflicts
  - Bullies on campus
  - Negative role models
  - Dysfunctional families
  - Political obstacles (underrepresented areas, low voter turnout)
  - The Target Population's cultural beliefs (e.g., some cultures have a stigma against mental health, thinking that if someone has a mental health problem they've been possessed by a spirit)
  - Gangs (threats, pressures to join, unsafe passage)
  - Doctors hesitant to treat members of the Target Population
  - Absentee fathers
  - Parents in denial (in juvenile hall, parents of repeat offenders for hellacious crimes often repeatedly say "but she's basically a good kid")
- **Individual (self-generated) conflict:** These are the ways your Target Population may be preventing themselves from achieving their overarching goal. In education, for example, individuals can impede their own progress or performance because of poor

135

attendance, bad behavior, low expectations, gender stereotypes, or poor resiliency skills. Here are examples of individual (self-generated) conflict I used in recent grant proposals:

- Language (barriers, literacy, proficiency)
- Lowered expectations (those in a re-training/ re-entry program were satisfied with a service job when they could be setting their sights on a profession)
- In the health field (fear of treatment, lack of physical activity, obesity, failure to follow-up on referrals, lack of insurance, distrust of "the system")
- Ignorance about existing area resources
- Absence of specific skills (life skills, resiliency, goal planning, study skills, test taking)
- Disabilities (physical, learning, language)

Option Two: Pinpointing the Gaps

If you can understand and apply this concept of addressing gaps then you've made the big leagues in terms of program design. Personally, I've used this concept in nine out of 10 of my program designs.

To best illustrate this concept of identifying and addressing gaps, think of your Target Population stopped on a road at the precipice of a canyon. Looking across that great, bottomless impassable chasm, your Target Population sees a road on the other side that leads to their destination. It's your Planning Team's job to build a bridge that could transport your Target Population from the road they are on to the road that could take them where they need to be.

Simply, gaps in services can be defined in three parts:

1. Your Target Population has a specific unmet need.
2. There are resources or services nearby that could meet your Target Population's needs.
3. There are no current means of bridging your Target Population with those needed resources.

Often you'll notice funding agency staff constantly begging grant applicants: "Don't reinvent the wheel." Translated that means they are asking you to: first, identify EXISTING gaps then; second, design a program that cleverly, economically and efficiently links your Target Population to those EXISTING resources.

Here are a few examples of a canyon-like gaps that existed between a Target Population and available resources/solutions.

- *Gap:* Despite a high rate of severe eye disease in infants within their county, an impoverished, isolated rural community lacked any ophthalmologists or sophisticated screening methods. Several hundred miles away in a major city, a research hospital operated an underused no-cost eye care program run by volunteer graduate students.

- **The bridge?** A remote medical camera set up at a local school in the rural community. A real-time video transmitted a high-definition image of a patient's eye to hospital specialists for a diagnosis.
- *Gap:* An overwhelmed, understaffed, adult literacy program lacks the funds to maintain the necessary inventory of multiple-level/multiple-language books. A local library is well stocked with these books but is open only a limited amount of hours because of budget cuts.
  - **The bridge?** A grant that provides regular transportation to the library for adults who will not only access books and materials, but volunteer in the library so it can stay open more hours.
- *Gap:* Third world countries where medical supplies and food are backlogged at warehouses while residents of remote local villages are slowly dying and starving to death.
  - **The bridge?** A grant that supplies locals with, and trains and pays them to operate, All-Terrain Vehicles to transport supplies to these villages.
- *Gap:* Parents who want to help their children learn to read by helping their child practice at home what they've learned in school—but their work schedule

doesn't permit them to visit the classroom during the day.

- **The bridge?** A grant that provides parents with videos of teachers reading stories to their class and, on-camera, sharing tips with parents.

Option Three:
Point-Of-View and Perception

Another way to think of conflict is from the point-of-view of all involved. Right or wrong, fair or unfair, fixable or unfixable, what would various sectors of your Target Population say is preventing them from achieving the Overarching Goal?

As an example of point-of-view, let's use the gang violence prevention program discussed in the Character chapter to identify the Conflict from the various points-of-view of those involved.

First, we would have to know the Target Population:

at-risk students

Next, the Overarching Goal of our hypothetical program design:

...to reduce the number of gang-related incidents of violence by at-risk students on district campuses

Then, you would ask your Planning Team and representative members of your Target Population: *from the Target*

Population's unique perspective what are some of the Whos and the Whats standing in the way of those at-risk students reaching their Overarching Goal?

- Intimidated students might say that gang pressure is so intense that it's easier and safer to join a gang.
- Overwhelmed parents might say they don't know how to spot the signs of gang involvement.
- Frustrated teachers might know they are able to help students but have no time within their daily instruction schedule.
- Local law enforcement officers might say the problem is the lack of positive role models for younger students who look up to gang members as heroes.
- Other points of view might come from younger, impressionable siblings of gang-involved students. Administrators would certainly have a take on the problem. What about school counselors? Local human service agency workers? Crime victims?

Problems of perception were discussed earlier in the Character chapters. How and why does your Target Population fail to address or acknowledge or perceive their problems and conditions? The reasons can be many: antiquated beliefs, cultural prejudices, fear and distrust of a system, or victims who are in denial. The example given earlier was a small community's distrust of the criminal justice process that makes them hesitant to report they have been victimized or witnessed crimes.

Wannabe Example of Step One:
Brainstorming

As we go through this process, we'll work with our friends at the Camp Wannabe Preschool Program. First, let's remind ourselves of their Overarching Goal:

> Improve the kindergarten readiness level of
> its graduates.

So the question that the Wannabe planning team should ask themselves is:

> What physical, internal and external obstacles
> stand in the way of our students improving
> their kindergarten readiness?

Here is the Camp Wannabe list of ideas after their brainstorming sessions. Read how varied Camp Wannabe's potential sources of conflict are. They range from lack of parking spaces to glare from the sun to more compensation for teachers. Some in the list are a little off target or redundant. That's okay. You may at first list many more obstacles than can possibly be tackled. That's okay too.

That's the process.

Conflict Worksheet #1 –
POTENTIAL CONFLICT

- We need more volunteers in the classroom
- There's not enough parking for parents
- There's no way for us to know if parents are doing what we ask them to do at home
- Students can't see the computer monitors because of the glare from the morning sun
- Can't attract better teachers without comparable pay rates
- The Program Director is not around to talk to staff after the students are dismissed
- Parents are concerned about safety because it's a bad neighborhood
- Some students still haven't had eye exams
- Students aren't eating their breakfasts and they can't learn on an empty stomach
- There are no incentives for parents to come to meetings or training sessions
- There's a major scheduling quandary—parents have erratic schedules at night and there's no time in the day for more activities
- Student language barriers
- Few bilingual staff
- Budget cuts
- Reduction of Early Reader Resources Specialist hours at school
- No formal professional development
- Lack of family support
- No parent outreach activities

- No early morning activities scheduled when most parents can attend
- Teachers need training about methods of instruction that can be used to make students more kindergarten-ready and teachers need training that focuses on working with parents so parents can support school activities and reinforce learning in their own homes
- There are not enough current materials that reflect the gender, culture, and ethnicity of our families
- The instructional equipment used (computers, listening posts, etc.) is outdated and usually not working properly
- Parents have difficulty getting to these resources because of their erratic schedules
- Better coordination of activities with current kindergarten practices
- More focused time needs to be spent on literacy activities during the instructional day
- Get more fathers involved, 95% of mothers doing all the work
- Books get ripped and damaged too easily
- More read-along CDs needed
- Testing takes up too much staff time
- Parents need to be able to manage their children before they can help them learn
- Parent teacher conferences need to be held more frequently and be more constructive
- Teachers need incentives to participate in additional training
- Professional training is too basic for the experienced staff and too advanced for new staff
- Extra instruction time is needed for students with learning disabilities

- Students who enter school in the middle of the year can't catch up
- Parents don't understand the importance of early literacy
- None of the school materials can be checked out for home use
- School fences are in disrepair
- The loudspeakers are too loud in the playground
- Planes from the airport fly over too low and are too loud
- Some parents refuse to pay for learning materials

STEP TWO:
WEEDING OUT

Wannabe staff brainstormed and collected way-too-long lists of possible points of conflict—some of which are insightful and others that are irrelevant or not realistic. Now is the time to weed out the extraneous.

Which are extraneous? Those ideas and suggestions that don't immediately and directly have to do with the Overarching Goal of the Target Population.

Eliminate those.

Remember, you're focusing on the WHAT and WHO that are in the way of the Target Population achieving their Overarching Goal.

Here is the Camp Wannabe list after this weeding out was completed.

Conflict Worksheet #2 – WEEDING OUT

- ~~There's not enough parking for parents~~
  ➥ *This one is about parent needs, not children's*

- Students can't see the computer monitors because of the glare from the morning sun

- ~~Planes from the airport fly over too low and are too loud~~
  ➥ *This has to do with the airport, not Camp Wannabe*

- There are not enough current materials that reflect the gender, culture, and ethnicity of our families

- The instructional equipment used (computers, listening posts, etc.) is outdated and usually not working properly

- Books get ripped and damaged too easily

145

- ~~The loudspeakers are too loud in the playground~~
  - ➥ *This is more a gripe rather than an obstacle to achieving the overarching goal.*
- More read-along CDs needed
- More bilingual materials needed at various levels
- None of the school materials can be checked out for home use
- ~~School fences are in disrepair~~
  - ➥ *This is about safety, not improving kindergarten readiness levels.*
- There's no way for us to know if parents are doing what we ask them to do at home
- There are no incentives for parents to come to meetings or training sessions
- ~~Some parents refuse to pay for learning materials~~
  - ➥ *This is about parents not the children. Also, the grant will pay for materials so that alone cancels this one out.*
- Lack of family support
- No parent outreach activities
- Parents have difficulty getting to these resources because of their erratic schedules
- Get more fathers involved, 95% of mothers doing all the work
- ~~Parents need to be able to manage their children before they can help them learn~~
  - ➥ *This one is more about parents learning parenting skills, not helping their children academically.*
- Parent teacher conferences need to be held more frequently and be more constructive
- Parents don't understand the importance of early literacy

- ~~Can't attract better teachers without comparable pay rates~~
  - ➡ *The focus should be improving the skills of existing teachers not recruiting new teachers.*
- ~~The Program Director is not around to talk to staff after the students are dismissed~~
  - ➡ *This sounds more like a workplace complaint. If however, the complaint was that the Program Director should communicate with Camp Wannabe staff about ways of improving student performance, then it would be a keeper.*
- Few bilingual staff
- Staff are not as aware of cultural issues as they should be
- Reduction of "Early Reader Resources Specialist" hours at school
- Teachers need training about methods of instruction that can be used to make students more kindergarten-ready
- Teachers don't have training that focuses on working with parents so parents can support school activities and reinforce learning in their own homes
- Teachers don't have any incentives to participate in additional training
- Professional training is too basic for the experienced staff and too advanced for new staff
- Student language barriers
- Some students still haven't had eye exams
- Students aren't eating their breakfasts and they can't learn on an empty stomach
- Students who enter school in the middle of the year can't catch up
- ~~Budget cuts~~
  - ➡ *This is too general and about something beyond the control of staff*

- There's a major scheduling quandary—parents have erratic schedules at night and there's no time in the day for more activities
- ~~No formal professional development program~~
  ➡ *While this is relevant, it is too general a statement. Other comments in this area are more specific.*
- We need more volunteers in the classroom
- ~~Parents are concerned about safety because it's a bad neighborhood~~
  ➡ *While no one would ever dismiss the importance of safety, it is not about the overarching goal.*
- No early morning activities scheduled when most parents could attend
- No coordination of activities with current kindergarten practices
- More focused time needs to be spent on literacy activities during the instructional day
- ~~Testing takes up too much staff time~~
  ➡ *A good point but one that hints at eliminating a component (assessment) that is necessary to the operation and funding of Camp Wannabe.*
- Extra instruction time is needed for students with learning disabilities

STEP THREE:
GROUPING AND PRIORITIZING

From those remaining on your list, group related Conflict into generalized categories. To simplify the process, limit yourself to no more than five of these general categories: In the Wannabe example these are (1) students, (2) parents, (3) facilities, (4) alternative activities and (5) prevention education.

What if you have less than five generalized categories? Four is good. Three is passable. Less than three and there's a problem with your list of Conflict not being varied enough. Three to five generalized categories is the ideal.

Conflict Worksheet #3 - GROUPING

GROUPING #1: CONFLICT RELATING TO INADEQUATE FACILITIES AND MATERIALS

- Students can't see the computer monitors because of the glare from the morning sun
- There are not enough current materials that reflect the gender, culture, and ethnicity of our families
- The instructional equipment (computers, listening posts, etc.) is outdated and usually not working properly
- Books get ripped and damaged too easily
- More read-along CDs are needed
- More bilingual materials are needed
- None of the school materials can be checked out for home use

GROUPING #2: CONFLICT RELATING TO LACK OF PARENT/FAMILY INVOLVEMENT

- There is no way for us to know if parents are doing what we ask them to do at home
- There are no incentives for parents to come to meetings or training sessions
- Lack of family support
- No parent outreach activities
- Parents have difficulty getting to these resources because of their erratic schedules
- Get more fathers involved, it's 95% of mothers doing all the work
- Parent teacher conferences need to be held more frequently and be more constructive
- Parents don't understand the importance of early literacy

GROUPING #3: CONFLICT RELATING TO UNPREPARED TEACHERS AND STAFF

- Few bilingual staff
- Staff are not as aware of cultural issues as they should be
- Reduction of "Early Reader Resources Specialist" hours at school
- Teachers need training about methods of instruction that can be used to make students more kindergarten-ready
- Teachers don't have training that focuses on working with parents so parents can support school activities and reinforce learning in their own homes

- Teachers don't have any incentives to participate in additional training
- Professional training is too basic for the experienced staff and too advanced for new staff

GROUPING #4: CONFLICT RELATING TO STUDENT LEARNING BARRIERS

- Student language barriers
- Some students still haven't had eye exams
- Students aren't eating their breakfasts and they can't learn on an empty stomach
- Students who enter school in the middle of the year can't catch up

GROUPING #5: CONFLICT RELATING TO OPERATIONS AND INSTRUCTION

- There is a major scheduling quandary—parents have erratic schedules at night and there is no time in the day for more activities
- We need more volunteers in the classroom
- No early morning activities scheduled when most parents can attend
- No coordination of activities with current kindergarten practices
- More focused time needs to be spent on literacy activities during the instructional day
- Extra instruction time is needed for students with learning disabilities

STEP FOUR:
SUMMARIZING

Next, you're going to turn the final three to five general areas of conflict into one-sentence summaries. Remember, here—and in all the other steps—continue to focus, combine and refine your ideas and summaries by making sure they are about the Target Population achieving the Overarching Goal.

For example, look at the first general area of conflict in the Grouping Worksheet #1, under "Conflict Relating To Inadequate Facilities And Materials." There are seven specific supporting points. Now summarize those points into one sentence, keeping it about the Target Population achieving the Overarching Goal. Your task is to adequately cover all seven supporting points and summarize them as a whole:

> Area #1: Student learning materials are not accessible, age-appropriate or maintained properly.

The other general areas of conflict and supporting points could be summarized as follows:

> Area #2: Parents are unaware of the importance of their involvement in their children's learning at school and in the home.

Area #3: Teachers need more training about how to deal with the cultural issues and learning challenges facing the changing Target Population.

Area #4: Students need help to overcome obstacles to learning that are unrelated to learning disabilities.

Area #5: The school schedule needs to be restructured to allow teachers more time for training, quality teaching time, and to provide parents with structured opportunities for classroom involvement.

Take a moment to review the summaries above.

Together, the five tell a pretty comprehensive story. We've taken complex, comprehensive lists of conflicts and summarized each down to one sentence. The result? Camp Wannabe clearly knows areas in which they need improvement if they are to achieve their Overarching Goal.

Remember that this process won't be easy. It may take several passes, many rewrites and a lot of time.

✛ ✛ ✛

The program you design will address those three to five areas of conflict and unmet needs summarized for your specific Target Population. This will result in positive changes that will empower your Target Population to achieve their Overarching Goal.

Positive change is what the next "C" of *Jon's Almost World Famous Seven Cs!* is about.

Chapter 2-12

Movies, For A Change
A VISIT WITH PHIL N. LeBLANC

Now that we've spent a few dozen chapters together and had an honest, productive exchange of ideas, this is a good time for us to talk frankly about something—the cleansing of your bowels.

Perhaps I should explain.

I'm talking about the *figurative* bowels of your main character.

If you look at the etymology of the word "catharsis" you'll find that the literal meaning translates roughly into the cleansing of one's innards, or bowels.

So, whether it's called "catharsis" or the "character's arc," in terms of screenwriting we know that change refers to the main character going through:

- An emotional gut-wrenching
- A traumatic event
- A psychological breakthrough, or
- A showdown with her/his own demons

We're talking about a wholesale change in a character's constitution as a result of the unfolding events of the story.

Screenwriting Axiom #11

If The Events Of The Story Do Not Change Your Character, Then Change Your Story

From preschool on, how many times have we heard a story end with, "...and the moral of the story is..."? An audience likes a character who learns something. If screenwriters are doing their jobs, the audience is transposed inside the mind of the characters. And when the audience gets in the mind of the characters what they're thinking to themselves is, "I wish I could do or say that" or "If I were in that character's circumstances I'd like to think that I'd do the same." And if a character changes for the better then maybe way down deep inside it gives us (the audience) hope that, "Well if s/he can learn and become a better person, then maybe there's hope for me."

Another important reason for change is that each time a character changes, for better or worse, another layer to the character's personality is added or exposed. This layering of traits and dimensions is what causes the character to develop over the course of the story—and become someone the audience knows, empathizes with and roots for.

Change And That Other "C"

This "C," CHANGE, is directly tied into another of *Jon's Almost World Famous Seven Cs!*. Can you guess which?

C'mon try.

Which other "C" does Change directly relate to?

Here's a not-so-subtle hint: we're talking about change in a character's *emotional/psychological* constitution. And when we talk about the buried emotional/psychological state of a character we usually think of ...?

CRISIS. Here's how CHANGE and CRISIS are tied together.

Remember the example of *Rocky*? The movie is NOT about Rocky going toe-to-toe with the champion, but instead going toe-to-toe with his own self-doubts and biggest fears. The fact that he's a bum wallowing in self pity, too afraid to try and do anything about it, is his emotional/psychological Crisis. Rocky falling in love, going the distance, and finding the "eye of the tiger" is overcoming his Crisis and, as a result, changing.

Screenwriting Axiom #12

The Ultimate Change Should Be A Result Of The Character's Initiative

When it comes to change, the main character should not be sitting on the sidelines watching and reacting to another character deciding the outcome for her/him. Instead, s/he should be proactive; making the change, whether it's by choice or by circumstances.

Often in movies the final climax revolves around the main character backed into a psychologically traumatic corner and faced with a moral dilemma—a difficult, if not impossible, choice. Often, it's choosing between saving her/himself or sacrificing her/himself to save others. Whatever the specific choices, it's important to remember as a storyteller that the more difficult the choice and the more it is embedded with emotion and deals with the character's Crisis, the better the story. Often, the entire story builds up to this choice.

Think of *Sophie's Choice* where Sophie, imprisoned with her two children in a Nazi concentration camp, is forced by a sadistic guard to make the harrowing choice of deciding which one of her two children will live and which will die.

Think of *Casablanca* where Rick, Mr. Doesn't-Stick-His-Neck-Out-For-Anyone, is faced with two impossible choices: helping Ilsa, his long lost love, escape safely with her new love or turning Ilsa's new love in to the authorities and having a heartbroken Ilsa all to himself.

A Visit With Our Old Friend, Phil N. LeBlanc

As with most storytellers, screenwriters work to get it right before they write. That's why it is important for them to determine how the character is going to change at the end of a story before they start writing.

One way to do this is as simple as filling in the blanks by answering this question in just a few words:

The character changes from ____?____ to ____?____ .

For example, Rick in Casablanca changes from selfish to self-sacrificing.

Often the change is a 180-degree reversal. A character may go from:

Greedy to giving.

Unsure to confident.

Afraid of women to head-over-heels in love.

Change doesn't always have to be positive. It can be:

From powerful to powerless.

From free to imprisoned.

From successful to broke.

Seem simple? That's what it should be.

But the process of honing in on the specific words is an important step in clarifying to the screenwriter what his/her story is really about and how the character changes (again, think: emotion and psychological resonance).

There Will Be Some Changes Made

Whether the character changes for the better or worse is up to the individual storyteller and the type of story s/he chooses to tell. Whatever the decision, the change (or lack of change) should:

- Be difficult
- Result in the character never being the same
- Have "do-or-die" type consequences, and
- Have emotional/psychological resonance

The lesson learned here by screenwriters and storytellers is that character change, when executed well, has more emotional impact on the audience than the biggest and loudest pyrotechnics, any stunt-filled chase, or any computer-generated battle scene.

So, have you learned anything from this chapter? Do you think you as a writer—and your writing—will change as a result of being more aware of this "C"? Good. Consider your bowels cleansed.

There are also lessons to be learned here for your Planning Team. As you will read in the next chapter, the success of your program design will be measured by how your Target Population has the potential to change.

Chapter 2-13

Change In Program Design
A FINISH LINE

In terms of program design, your change will not be as philosophical or thematic as it is in screenwriting. Rather, the Change you propose for your Target Population should be mostly quantitative—tangible and measurable.

In the chapters about Conflict (2–10 and 2–11) we categorized three to five areas of your Target Population's conflict or unmet needs, then summarized each into a sentence.

Change in program design is the result of how you plan to achieve your Overarching Goal by addressing each of those summarized categories of Conflict.

But, be warned: While the final results of this chapter may look simple, formulating and phrasing these changes is a complex process of continually simplifying, revising and refocusing. The benefit from this continual process of focusing and phrasing will lead to your program design being better focused and phrased.

STEP ONE: GOALS

The first step in this process is to turn each of your one-sentence summaries of conflict into a goal; changing the summaries from pointing out *what is wrong* to *what needs to be addressed.*

To create a goal, we first ask this question about each one-sentence summary:

"In very general terms, what long-term anticipated change (results or consequences) do you want to achieve?"

To answer that, remember goals are an ultimate destination—a finish line:

G—is for general
O—is for overarching
A—is for all-encompassing
L —is for long-term

When it comes to the phrasing of your goals, we'll use the same five-point inspection that we used for the Overarching Goal:

1) Does your goal start with a positive active verb?
2) Does your goal avoid the "A-" word?
3) Does your goal mention solutions?
4) Is your goal twenty words or less?
5) Is your goal measurable?

A Wannabe Goal

Using the work we did with the Camp Wannabe Preschool Program as an example, we're going to transform one summarized area of conflict into one program goal. Here's one of Camp Wannabe's areas of conflict as summarized in the Conflict chapter:

> Parents are unaware of the importance of their involvement in their children's learning at school and in the home.

Remember the five-point inspection, we want to start our goal with a positive action verb. In this case, "Increase."

Version One: *Goal One:* Increase parent awareness about the importance of their involvement in their children's learning at school and in the home.

In reading the above—and thinking of a goal as stating our ultimate destination—I realized that the "finish line" is not to just make parents *more aware.* Increasing awareness is a step in that direction but not the ultimate goal. Instead, the ultimate destination (goal) is to get parents *more involved.* Also, involvement is more measurable (tangible) than awareness (a frame of mind). So, let's rephrase it with a new emphasis on involvement:

Version Two: *Goal One:* Increase parent involvement
                 in their children's learning at school and
                 in the home.

That's much better. Let's take it through the five-point inspection.

Action/improvement verb? "Increase…"

Is there an "and?" Actually there is, which tells us that the goal does not have a singular focus. We'll go back and take out the "and" when we do "Revision #3."

Is a solution mentioned? No. That's good.

Short and sweet? 13 words. Under 20.

Measurable? If we're talking about parents spending time in the classroom and at home applying the principles, then those are measurable.

So one more pass should do it if we take out the "and":

Version Three: *Goal One:* Increase parent involvement
                 in their children's learning.

That's a well-phrased goal. By taking out the entire phrase that contained "and," we eliminated specifics and stated what we want to accomplish in the most general of terms.

Now use this same process for each of your summarized areas of conflict. When you're done, you have the Overarching Goals of your Program Design. Here are the rest of Camp Wannabe's goals:

1) Provide students more access to age-appropriate learning materials.

2) Increase parent involvement in their children's learning.

3) Train teachers to incorporate a culturally sensitive curriculum that incorporates parent support as a tool to improving students' kindergarten readiness.

4) Reduce the number of socio-economic obstacles to learning specific to Wannabe students and their families.

5) Provide teachers and parents with ample time, space and state-of-the-art learning tools to improve students' kindergarten readiness levels.

No More, No Less

We've heard seasoned grant writers say that "the right number of goals" for a typical grant application should be three.

First, beware of writers who refer to themselves as "seasoned." Seasonings were invented to preserve tasteless, old meat.

Second, there is no right number. When it comes to objectives, your program design should have—as Mozart said about musical notes in his works in *Amadeus*—"...just as many that are needed, no more, no less...."

STEP TWO: OBJECTIVES

Goals state what you want to accomplish in the most *general* of terms.

Objectives break down each generalized program goal into *specific* areas of focus that detail exactly WHAT will be achieved and WHEN it will be achieved.

To determine if each objective statement is formulated and phrased properly, here are five key questions each of your objectives should answer:

1) **WHO is expected to change or benefit?**
2) **WHAT (measurable) change or benefit is expected?**
3) **HOW much change is expected or HOW many will benefit?**
4) **WHEN is the change or benefit expected to happen?**
5) **As measured by...?**

Your aim is to write objectives that are SMART:
- **S – specific**
- **M – measurable**
- **A – achievable**
- **R – reachable**
- **T – time-locked**

Here a Verb, There A Verb ...

Remember *what* should change: knowledge, abilities, skills, health status, behavior, income, circumstances or status—anything measurable or demonstrable.

Measurable action verbs often used include improve, decrease, reduce, expand, demonstrate, participate, etc.

Avoid using lofty, esoteric, touchy-feely phrases that are impossible to measure or prove such as "Heighten the awareness of ...", "Will become more sensitive to...", "Will gain a better sense of..."

I'm 100% Sure Of This

Salvador Dali once said, "have no fear of perfection, you'll never reach it."

No Reader/Scorer expects your program design to be perfect. For a variety of reasons (e.g., illness, schedules, transportation), upon implementation of your proposed program, not all participants will be in attendance at every activity. For example, every day in local schools, the absence rate can be as high as 15%. Because of this, no Reader/Scorer expects 100% of your participants to reap 100% benefit from 100% of the services provided, 100% of the time.

Despite this, MOST objectives often read something like:

Version One: By the end of the year, 100% of all participants will participate in all family counseling sessions.

167

First, there are actually two "100%s" in the above example: "100% of all participants..." and "all (i.e., 100%) family counseling sessions." So, the objective is unrealistic and not well thought out.

To create an achievable objective, revise the 100% into a more realistic and achievable percentage:

Version Two: By the end of the year, a minimum of 90% of all participants will complete a minimum of 20 out of 25 family counseling sessions.

As Measured By...

You will be required to prove any progress you make toward achieving an objective. This will require some form of a measurement tool that measures quantitative or qualitative results.

Basically, a quantitative measure involves numbers. Examples of quantitative measurement tools include: attendance reports, test scores, number of services provided, and assessment scales.

Qualitative measures do not involve numbers. Qualitative measurement tools can include: observations, attitudinal surveys, focus group questions, opinion polls and participant reflections.

A complete objective should include the words "...as measured by..." Although you are sure to use multiple measurement tools, include a specific example of one measurement tool to be used.

"Something Remarkable"

"Don't live down to expectations," said playwright Wendy Wasserstein, "Go out there and do something remarkable." When it comes to deciding what will be achieved in the objectives, there is no "right" number of objectives, only realistic and doable numbers determined by your Planning Team's knowledge of, and experiences providing services to, your Target Population.

Remember, the Reader/Scorer has more than likely been in your shoes and has a good idea of what is realistic and doable.

But also remember, Reader/Scorers look for a program that intends to do "something remarkable."

Because of this, I strongly feel that you can, and should, impress a Reader/Scorer by setting the bar as high as possible—*as long as common sense (and perhaps a lie detector) tells you that, if all goes well, the objective's expectation is attainable.* It's a way of selling the fact that you are confident in your staff's ability to accomplish the task.

Writing The Objectives:
Another Wannabe Example

When designing your program, create several specific objectives that branch out from each of the generalized goals. Let's use a Wannabe goal as an example to create a set of sample objectives.

First, the goal:

Goal One: Increase parents' involvement in their children's learning.

Accomplishing this goal will require several areas of focus designed to address the conflicts and unmet needs listed under the general area of parents from our work in Chapter 2-11—Conflict. The Planning Team decides that the areas of focus to accomplish the goal of increasing parent involvement should include:

1) Conducting an outreach/education campaign to educate parents about the importance of being involved in their children's learning at school and at home.

2) Setting up a program with incentives that motivates parents to volunteer in their child's classroom.

3) Providing parent education classes that demonstrate ways for parents to reinforce student learning at home.

Okay, three areas of focus needed to accomplish the first goal. The next step is to transform each of these areas of focus into an objective. Let's tackle the third from the list above and write an objective that addresses it. First step, answer the five key questions about the task.

1. WHO is expected to change or benefit?

Although the children will ultimately benefit from this objective, it's the parents who will be expected to change.

2. WHAT (measurable) change or benefit is expected?

Based on our answer above, we know to answer this one in terms of the parents. So what is the specific change we want in parents? From the classes we provide, we want parents to learn methods of reinforcing what students learn in the classroom, at home. This can be measured in the number of parents that complete the class and increases in the amount of work completed by families at home.

3. HOW MUCH change is expected or HOW MANY will benefit?

This is about the "What?" in #2 above. So, how many parents do we want to complete the parent involvement class? In the first year, if we can get 20% of our 300 parents to complete the class, that would be a manageable number and make an impact—so, 60 parents.

4. WHEN is the change or benefit expected to happen?

For this example, let's assume we're talking about the first year of a multi-year grant. When should the completion of these parent classes occur? Common sense tells us *before* the beginning of the school year so parent contributions can be applied to the classroom from day one.

5. As measured by...

Upon completing all requirements of this class, parents will receive a completion certificate that entitles them to a parent handbook or video.

Now that all the basics are laid out in the answers above, let's assemble those answers to write our first version of the objective. Let's also keep in mind that, like a pile of clay on a potter's wheel, it's going to take awhile to shape this objective and get it right.

Version One: *Objective:* Prior to the beginning of the school year, 60 parents will complete a class to learn methods of reinforcing student classroom learning in their home, as measured by completion certificates.

Stop and take another look at this first pass at the objective. It's good enough for MOST designs, but not for ours.

Why? Objectives are about being as specific as possible and demonstrating to the Reader/Scorer that we have thought this out, done our homework and are ready to launch the program as soon as we get the award.

So, let's be more specific and show the Reader/Scorer we've done our homework.

They "will complete a class" means what? *Quantify everything.* For this example, "complete" will mean that they will complete a 10-hour training.

And let's be even *more* specific (you knew I was going to suggest that...right?). Let's not refer to it as "a class" but instead by the proper name of the class because that will specify the focus of the curriculum and "artfully sell" exactly what we're doing. For this example the name of the curriculum might be "The Parent Partnership." So we'll refer to it as "the Parent Partnership class" rather than "the class."

Version Two: *Objective:* Prior to the beginning of the school year, 60 parents will complete a 10-hour Parent Partnership class to learn methods of reinforcing student classroom learning in their home, as measured by completion certificates.

Reads well and more focused, except for one thing—the "60 parents" number. Is that enough? We're not sure. While we don't want to commit to a concrete number over 60, more parents could possibly complete the class. So let's avoid committing to a hard number and make the number a minimum, implying that more parents could be accommodated.

Version Three: *Objective:* Prior to the beginning of the school year, a minimum of 60 parents will complete a 10-hour Parent Partnership class to learn methods of reinforcing student classroom learning in their home, as measured by completion certificates.

Okay, we're satisfied with this objective.

But let's verify that our new and improved objective answers the five key questions for objectives:

- **WHO** is expected to change or benefit?
  Parents

- **WHAT** (measurable) change or benefit is expected?
  Methods of reinforcing student classroom learning in their home

- **HOW MUCH** change or benefit is expected?
  ...a minimum of 60 parents will learn...

- **WHEN** is the change or benefit expected to happen?
  Prior to the beginning of the school year

- **As measured by...?**
  Completion certificates

Numbering The Goals And Objectives

To keep your design orderly and easier for the Reader/Scorer to follow, come up with a clear and consistent method of numbering your goals and objectives. Here's one I use.

First, number the goals. The example from Camp Wannabe above would be written as:

> *Goal One:* Increase parents' involvement in their children's learning.

Second, number each objective under Goal One. The first would be labeled "Objective 1-1"; that is Goal One – Objective One. This would be written as:

Objective 1-1: Prior to the beginning of the school year, a minimum of 60 parents will complete a 10-hour Parent Partnership class to learn methods of reinforcing student classroom learning in their home, as measured by completion certificates.

The second objective under Goal One (i.e., Goal One— Objective Two) would be written as:

Objective 1-2: Increase the number of....

Combined, the goal and objectives would be laid out as shown below. It's easy-on-the-eye and easy to follow.

GOAL ONE: Increase parents' involvement in their children's learning.
- *Objective 1-1:* By the third month of each school year, a minimum of 90% of all parents will complete and sign a checklist of steps and activities they have taken to become more involved in their children's learning at school and at home.

- *Objective 1-2:* At the end of each school year, the number of parents who receive incentives that result in their attending a classroom volunteer orientation will increase by a minimum of 20%, as measured by sign-in sheets.

- *Objective 1-3:* Prior to the beginning of the school year, a minimum of 60 parents will complete a 10-hour Parent Partnership Protocol class to learn methods of reinforcing student classroom learning in their home, as measured by completion certificates.

- *Objective 1-4:* By the end of the first school year, each classroom will have a roster of a minimum of six parents volunteering a minimum of once a month, as measured by parent sign-in sheets.

✛   ✛   ✛

As cautioned earlier, this is a process of writing, rewriting and rewriting some more. Remember to use the key questions for each objective as a guide to formulate and phrase.

Once you have created your list of goals and objectives, they will become, in essence, an outline for writing the details of your proposal.

So now the question becomes: How will each objective be accomplished and by whom? That is answered with the seventh of *Jon's Almost World Famous Seven Cs!*

Chapter 2-14

Collaboration In Movies
"PACKAGING"

When teaching creative writing and, more specifically, about the basic building blocks of story structure, I usually stop with the Sixth C.

But, for the purposes of program design there is a bonus "C"—COLLABORATION.

That's not to say collaboration is not an integral part of making movies. Screenwriting is especially known for its writing-by-committee nature. A screenwriter who is a hired gun and paid by a studio also answers to the studio. Because of this, s/he spends time in countless story meetings with countless studio executives. These are followed by countless meetings where s/he is in close collaboration with countless influential creative players that have a vested interest in the movie's outcome. In fact, for most screenwriters it is a struggle to escape these countless collaborators and carve out a few precious hours of daily respite to focus on the task that really counts—writing.

Agents and producers team up creative types—so called "bankable" or "A List" names—to collaborate on projects and present to studios an offer they can't refuse. This is the process of "packaging" a dream team of creative types in front of and behind the camera who have a history of successes, in hopes of reducing the likelihood of box office failure.

So now, onto the bonus "C" of *Jon's Almost World Famous Seven Cs!* where we find out that program design requires its own version of "packaging." While this is the last "C," it is by no means the least, so please read on.

Your life may depend on it.

Chapter 2-15

Collaboration In Program Design
A Matter Of Life Or Death

MOST of you wily veteranos have read the topic heading of this chapter and muttered something like:

"I already know all about collaboratives…"

or

"We're already doing that collaborating stuff…"

or

"Working with other programs or agencies is more trouble than it's worth…"

And that's great news for me!

That is, great news for me if we're competing against each other for the same grant funds. The intention of this chapter is to make clear a point that is so important it could be a matter of life or death—for your program design:

Ultimately, the process of designing an excellent program is really the process of building a new, or expanding an existing, collaborative.

Regardless of your experience with other programs or agencies, or your track record winning grants, your approach to each program design *should be*:

- This is our *new and improved* way we plan to collaborate for this specific proposed program;
- This is how we intend to collaborate *over and above* what we've done or are already doing; and,
- This is how *each new partner* will take our program design to the next level.

First: The Basics

Let's start with differentiating between two words often misused in grant applications. Often, applicants will mistakenly write "…we are forming a collaboration…" What they really mean to write is "…we are forming a collaborative…" What the collaborative does should be referred to as collaboration.

Huh? Let's try that again.

"Collaborative" is the noun: the group of experts, Community Based Organizations (CBOs) and community stakeholders formed to implement your program. Depending on the funding agency, a collaborative might also be referred to as a "partnership," "planning team," "your organization," "advisory board," "leadership team," "consortium" or "coalition."

"Collaboration" (Latin meaning: "work together") is the verb, what your collaborative does: pooling resources, communicating and working together to help your Target Population access services and achieve their Overarching Goal.

Second: A Little Marriage Counseling

Just because a collaborative looks good on paper, your job is far from done. In fact, all collaboratives work perfectly on paper but MOST collaboratives fall short in their execution. Any collaborative (i.e., mutually shared decision-making process) is always a work-in-progress.

Cheryl Gourgouris, a brilliant associate of mine who works as Director of Programs at a preeminent community-based organization (the Richstone Family Center), once compared collaboratives to marriages: Just because you exchange vows doesn't mean the hard part is done and the work in your relationship is over. She went on to suggest that in a collaborative, as in a marriage, when partners can talk about and share money without arguing, then you know you really have a partnership going.

FIVE REASONS WHY A COLLABORATIVE MAKES YOUR PROGRAM MORE EFFICIENT

Reason #1 – The Lead Agency

A collaborative provides leadership structure for your program through a lead agency, the chief Community Based Organization (CBO) or organization legally responsible for all financial and operational aspects of the grant. The lead agency needs to be eligible to apply for the grant based on the parameters set by the funding agency. A lead agency provides leadership, experience, expertise, and resources. It liaisons with the funding agency and is responsible for submission of all reports, budgets and audits. However, a lead agency does not necessarily have to oversee the day-to-day details of program operations.

So, a lead agency must be on solid financial ground. Your lead agency must have the capacity to manage the financial aspects of the grant award including: strong accounting operations, the ability to operate/carry the program in arrears if necessary, and providing accurate financial reports and audits.

If several partner agencies are on financially solid ground, have a great track record and are experienced at implementing grant-funded programs, how is the lead agency decided? Do all the partner reps put their foot in a circle and one starts with "...eenie, meenie, minie moe..."?

There are other ways.

Often, it is a matter of which partner first found the grant then called the meeting.

In other cases, the funding agency might award more points if the lead agency is located within the target area. In that case, the agency closest in proximity to the target area and target population wins.

Or, it comes down to who has the most experience with the target population and which agency staff best reflects the population to be served.

Sometimes the funding agency will mandate the exact agency they want to take the lead (e.g., a school district or community-based health clinic).

Reason #2 – The Advisory Board

The goals of partners and stakeholders in a collaborative are:

Cooperation

Communication

Continuity

The most efficient conduit for this is a program-specific advisory board created to oversee the start-up, operation and monitoring of your proposed program. But don't confuse this advisory board with a pre-existing Board of Directors from one of the partner agencies. Nor should you think that a mere listing of collaborating partners will do. From the outset, view your program-specific advisory board as an active, and interactive, leadership team chaired by a lead agency representative or the proposed program's coordinator. At a minimum, the Advisory Board should be made up of:

- One key representative from each partner agency,
- Community stakeholder representatives,
- Experts in the field, and
- Representatives from each sector of the target population.

In many programs, an expanded version of the planning team becomes the advisory board.

Reason #3 – A Concerted Outreach Campaign

Your advisory board can orchestrate a social marketing campaign that incorporates the same cutting edge marketing principles used to sell commercial products.

But instead of reaping profits, your collaborative's successful social marketing campaign will: increase your Target Population's, and the public's, awareness of the problem your program is addressing, change attitudes, and generate positive word-of-mouth within your Target Population. Beyond that, your collaborative's smart social marketing can result in community ownership of a problem. Experts in your collaborative will know:

- What type of marketing and materials pique your Target Population's interest
- The best way to educate the community about critical issues
- How to skew outreach efforts to specific target area demographic populations and their specific issues (e.g., various ages, gender-specific issues, social stigmas)
- How best to involve your Target Population's representatives in your outreach plan

Here are some specific examples of elements in a social marketing campaign for a program I designed:

- Posters and announcements in the lobby and entryway of each collaborating agency's sites

- Distributing multi-lingual flyers to families through students at each of the schools in the target area
- Announcements and news of activities and accomplishments included in partner newsletters and activity calendars
- Printing and distributing handbooks (in appropriate languages and literacy levels) outlining program policies and procedures and staff contact information
- Publicizing the program at school and community events (e.g., an annual community health fair)
- A 24-hour information hot line
- Updating relevant community and school committees and councils about the program's progress
- Creating and maintaining a website to document program progress and archive all relevant materials
- Scheduling activities to accommodate the schedules of your Target Population
- Holding an annual stakeholder meeting (at night so more will attend) to gather feedback and discuss all aspects of the program
- Cafecitos (informal morning coffees)
- Including announcements and information in utility bills

Reason #4 – Innovation

Most of the lauded grants I've been a part of involved the collaboration of two or more agencies that had never worked together. In some cases, we were cautioned by experts and naysayers that, in no uncertain terms, such an outside-the-box collaboration could not be done.

One example of this is the highly unlikely collaboration of a high school, a public transit agency and an employment development center. Inner-city high schoolers were getting into a lot of trouble and wasting a lot of time while waiting (sometimes for more than 90 minutes) in a bad area of town for their transfer bus. So three agencies were brought together to design a safe, supervised computer lab, learning center and job placement service for students. The site for this was not at the school but *inside the public transit center* where waiting for a bus and dodging bullets was transformed into a safe, supervised learning opportunity for students and a resource center for adults.

Reason #5 – Better Use of Evaluation Results

MOST program designs claim that their programs will be "data-driven;" that is, staff will collect, tabulate and analyze assessment and evaluation information to improve program services (aka "formative evaluation").

However, MOST programs fall short of this mark for four reasons. First, only a select few take the time to really analyze and consider the data. Second, too few staff are trained on how to fully understand the data then use the results to improve program delivery. Third, the results are rarely disseminated to all stakeholders for their consideration and feedback. Fourth, no regularly scheduled time is built into the program's schedules or meetings to discuss evaluation findings.

An advisory board—because all aspects of the program are represented by that body—is the ideal conduit to disseminate this information, receive feedback and develop a mechanism to ensure that feedback results in improved program delivery. Here is an example of how this process was described in a recent proposal:

> *Use of Data:* A goal of [the proposed program]
> is that the methods and tools used to monitor
> the project will be discreet enough, in data
> collected and frequency of collection, to
> determine at any point in time if project goals
> are being accomplished in a timely fashion.
> Collected data will be disseminated among
> members of the advisory board to generate
> their continued support and allow their
> expertise and efforts to continuously improve
> the program. In turn, each member of the
> advisory board will be charged with distributing
> results to those they represent, seeking
> feedback, and bringing the feedback back to
> the advisory board for reaction and action.
> Any necessary changes based on evaluation
> results will be developed and implemented by

the program within six weeks of the time the conclusive data was received. Summaries of all evaluation reports, in languages and literacy levels that reflect the population served, will be available on the program's Website or for review by anyone upon request.

FIVE REASONS WHY FUNDING AGENCIES OFTEN MANDATE COLLABORATION

Reason #1 - More Bang For Their Buck

Funding agencies do not want to see their money go to programs that work in isolation from, or in competition with, other nonprofits in your area with a similar purpose. The funding agency wants assurance that there have been discussions between your Planning Team and existing area programs—even if those programs are not part of your collaborative. To do this means your Planning Team, beginning in the planning phase, should reach out to other entities and invite their participation and input. These discussions could revolve around:

1) Where your proposed program fits within the context of services provided to the target area
2) Ways to cut costs by pooling resources and avoiding duplicative services
3) How to reach more of the target population that needs services
4) Sharing training expenses

5) Joint fundraising efforts
6) Deciding on future issues to be problem-solved
7) Coordinating social marketing efforts
8) Co-sponsoring community events and prevention/ education campaigns
9) Utilizing each other as referral sources
10) Sharing of data and coordinating evaluation activities

Reason #2 – Target Population Representation

The funding agency usually requires that your collaborative involve your Target Population in all aspects of your program. No matter how much experience your Planning Team has, no matter how much training and education your staff has received, no matter what your grant writer insists you include to win a grant and how you should word it, no one knows what your Target Population needs, or what will motivate your Target Population more, than your Target Population.

You need to—have to—MUST!—involve representatives from the population you intend to serve in all aspects of the process.

A collaborative is more impressive to the Reader/Scorer—and more efficient in the way it serves the target population—when the staff reflects, and is sensitive to the needs of, the target population it serves. The ethnicity, cultural make-up, and gender of your proposed program's advisory board and program staff should come as close as possible to reflecting the ethnicity, cultural make-up, and gender of the target population served.

Another way to do this is to staff your program with those who live—or grew up in—the target area or similar communities. You can also recruit staff with special training or credentials specific to working with the target population (e.g., sensitivity training, language classes, current social issues workshops). Or, if your grant involves education, hire staff/instructors trained in differentiated instruction strategies for various languages and ability levels.

Reason #3 – A Diversity Of Perspectives

A good collaborative will ensure a diversity of perspectives and equitable access in all aspects of your proposed program. "All aspects" includes planning, implementation, operation, monitoring, assessment, evaluation, and sustaining the program. A "diversity of perspectives" means:

- Formalizing an on-going method for gathering input from various ethnicities, genders and ages within your Target Population
- Soliciting input from those who may not be satisfied or disagree with the way the program is operated
- Including local cultural practices, alternative approaches and religious perspectives into service delivery

Reason #4 – Two-Way Communication

If all you intend to do with your program is feed your Target Population information and announcements and updates on what YOU think they should know and how YOU think the program is going without hearing from THEM—then YOU really aren't communicating.

Instead, what the Reader/Scorer is looking for are two-way—*repeat: two-way*—channels of communication and opportunities for feedback between your collaborative and your Target Population. Whether through e-mail, family meetings, luncheons, surveys, websites or newsletters, formal or informal gatherings—your Planning Team will know best how to reach your Target Population.

Take the proposed Camp Wannabe preschool grant as an example. *Formal* two-way communication might mean that on a regularly scheduled basis the Program Director has a morning coffee with parents to relay important information about the program and listen to parent concerns. *Informal* communication and exchanges of ideas might take place between teachers and parents as the children are dropped off and picked up each day. Here are just a few additional examples of how two-way communication could be further facilitated at Camp Wannabe:

- Target population representatives serving on the advisory board, committees and various task forces
- Program announcements, newsletters and informational e-mails created by and for the target population

- A website with a chat room
- A retreat with Target Population and partner representatives to discuss all aspects of program operations
- A video journal about your program on the local access channel
- Announcements included in utility bills sent to all families in the target area
- A participant phone tree
- CDs that, between songs used in the classroom, contain your marketing messages

Reason #5 – To Ensure Equitable Access

Equitable access in this case means that all who desire will have access to your proposed program services regardless of age, race, ethnicity, language, disability, or ability to pay. Examples of promoting equitable access include:

- Presenting all program materials in languages and literacy levels reflective of your Target Population
- Providing participants with disabilities special adaptive devices or other accommodations when appropriate
- Fostering appreciation of national origins through multicultural activities
- Creating activities that are age and culturally appropriate

- Providing translators who speak the various languages represented by the target population
- Abiding by all ADA accessibility guidelines required by the funding agency
- Demonstrating how you considered both genders in the design of the program
- Describing any existing policies and procedures that your partners have in place that mandate equitable access
- Describing how evaluation practices will be all-inclusive
- Ensuring that participant recruitment and outreach efforts connect with all strata of your Target Population
- Ensuring that all members of your Target Population have an opportunity to participate on the advisory board

FOUR REASONS WHY A COLLABORATIVE MAKES *CENTS*

Reason #1 – The Bottom Line

Alone, your agency or program may not have the resources, expertise or staff to provide all the services and overhead necessary to launch and sustain a grant-funded program. To do this, you and other programs will need to share costs and facilities. Or, the proposed program services may be so far-reaching and comprehensive that no one agency or program could possibly do it all.

For example, a local school district wants to provide comprehensive after school programming for at-risk youth. A local Mental Heath agency wants to provide counseling services to those youth. And, the local health department wants to provide health services to those high-risk families. Alone, there is no way that any of these three agencies could provide such a comprehensive array of services. In this case, the school district would be the fiscal agent for several reasons: (1) they are an eligible nonprofit, (2) are willing to absorb some administrative and start-up costs, (3) have a track record for providing exemplary extracurricular services and (4) have experience working with the state funding agency. As the lead agency, the school district would then subcontract with the health department and the mental health department to provide specific school site services.

The example above is a win-win situation for all. The funding agency gets more bang for their buck, the collaborative agencies receive additional money to provide much-need services and the target population is offered multiple services that theretofore did not exist.

Reason #2 – Your Agency Or Program Is The New Kid On The Block

Collaboration is good for an up and coming agency without a track record of winning grants or one that is new at operating a program. This is because another more experienced partner agency can serve as a financial guarantor.

Reason #3 – The Cash Or In-Kind Match Requirement

First, let's define the basic difference between an in-kind and cash match. More importantly, make sure you know *how the funding agency defines the difference* between the two.

➡ A **cash match** is a direct financial contribution to the total operating budget. This often occurs when an agency takes funds from another source (e.g., federal money, fundraisers, another grant) and applies it to the proposed program.

➡ Partners may make valued **in-kind contributions** in the form of anything but cash: that is, services, materials or facilities.

Here is an example of how I briefly described a partner match in a recent grant proposal for a Gear Up grant:

> Although Genericville is a small rural city, the school district has developed several collaborative relationships that have not only provided invaluable support in the past, but are now key supporters of this proposed GEAR UP program. These partners have been instrumental in designing the Genericville GEAR UP model, have helped in writing and preparing sections of this proposal, and are committed to its success. In addition to the school district's in-kind contribution of $177,136 over five years, partnering agencies are committing $844,167 over five years. This, coupled with the cash dollar-for-dollar match ($1,059,500) from student activities and family financial assistance, produces a grand total match over five years of $2,080,803—an 85% match over five years that exceeds GEAR UP requirements of at least a 50% match. [A brief description of each partner and their match followed.]

Reason #4 – Stopgap Funding

Funding and payment delays happen. This frequently occurs when the funding agency is a government entity with an annual budget dependent on legislative approval. If this should occur, *the buck will stop with you at the local level to maintain—and fund—the current level of services without a payment from the funding agency.*

Ouch!

Figure on the time that you might have to provide this stopgap funding to be approximately six to eight weeks. Your collaborative should be able to combine your resources and/or have enough of a financial reserve, emergency funds or line-of-credit to survive that six to eight week financial drought.

Your Local "Dream Team"

In your program design and proposal, present your collaborative as the most qualified, diverse and experienced team of local experts to provide the proposed services in your area. Beyond that, keep in mind that your collaborative's experience and qualifications will compete against other collaboratives' experiences and qualifications for grant awards. A few points to consider:

- Years of experience operating grant-funded programs and providing similar services to the target population
- The number of years your partners have collaborated
- Prior major accomplishments and awards received by your staff—even if those accomplishments and awards were earned before they arrived at your program

- Newspaper articles, funding agencies and politicians that have recognized the quality services your program/agency provides
- Any published, well-known experts in the field that may be part of your team
- The number of site visits to your program by prospective service providers using your practices as a model
- Any speaking engagements, presentations or workshops conducted by your staff at conferences or expos
- Any replicable intellectual property copyrighted or trademarked by your staff (e.g., evaluation templates, training materials, etc.)
- Staff who have been hired as consultants by other programs or agencies
- Unique, innovative, one-of-a-kind activities and events offered by your program
- Letters of support, thank you letters and testimonials from community stakeholders or program participants
- Any program-related specialized degrees or credentials earned by staff

And If You *Still* Don't Believe Me ...

I just randomly grabbed an RFP sitting on my desk and found the section that covers collaboration:

> *Partnerships (1½ pages):* Involvement of partners will substantially increase the likelihood of reaching project goals. List the primary partners in the collaborative, their relevant experience and their involvement in the planning and implementation process. The total score for this section is worth 20 out of a possible 100 points—or 20% of the total possible score.

This chapter should have helped you realize that no matter your budget, experience or track record:

1) Ultimately, the process of designing an excellent program is really the process of building a collaborative

2) Creating an innovative, effective collaborative requires a frame of mind that is set on delivering to the funding agency *more* than what you're already doing and *more* than what they are asking for

3) The stronger your collaborative—the stronger your program design

Chapter 3-1

A Great Program Name
YOU'LL KNOW IT WHEN YOU FEEL IT

Author of more than 100 books and screenplays, including *The Blackboard Jungle* and *The Birds*, Ed McBain (aka Evan Hunter) never started a novel until he was satisfied with the title. He would play around with words until he thought he stumbled upon the exact right order then change them, nudge them, polish them, test them on others and try the title in different fonts and colors.

Finally, he would hang the finished title up on his office wall. While writing, whenever he was in danger of losing track of the plot or straying from the story's theme, he'd ask himself, "What am I writing about?"

The answer was the perfect title that hung on his wall.

The late Broadway producer and playwright David Belasco's motto was, "If you can't write your idea on the back of [a] calling card, you don't have a clear idea."

In terms of marketing, the importance of a product name is immeasurable. Hundreds of millions of dollars are spent each year on "branding" to come up with the best combination of name, words and images that instantly identify a product and distinguish it from the competition.

Likewise, a great program name will heighten your Reader/ Scorer's expectations and *make a positive first impression.* The impression being that if you have carefully thought about your program name, chances are you will have also carefully thought out the rest of your program design.

Yet, as important as this is, MOST applicants spend only a few moments on their program's name. What they come up with is usually mediocre. As the saying goes, "Only mediocre writers are always at their best."

You'll Know It When You Feel It

So, there must be a fool-proof process—maybe even a magic formula—to come up with that one-in-a-million program name, right?

Wrong.

What is a great name for a program? No one knows, really. Some compare it with what a Supreme Court Justice said about obscenity, you'll know it when you see it.

I think it's slightly different with a great program name, you'll know it when you *feel* it.

What I mean by "feel" is that a great program name just clicks. Fits perfectly. Inspires. Seems so simple, so easy. Personally, I get goosebumps when I hear a great program name or a title—that's my gauge.

I also get jealous. If it's someone else's great program name I hear or read, I mutter to myself, "Why didn't I think of that?"

But don't plan on budgeting a certain amount of time to come up with a great program name. Sometimes, the program name may be the first thing you come up with. Other times, all will seem hopeless and it may take hours and hours. But your great program name is there. You'll find it.

Just trust the process.

COMMON CHARACTERISTICS OF A GREAT PROGRAM NAME

While a great program name can't be defined because it is so subjective, there are common characteristics of great program names to consider:

Tells The Story

A great program name can embrace the intrinsic nature and overarching goal of a program:

➥ *Success By Six* clearly captures the scope of United Way's early childhood coalitions focused on improving school readiness through community change.

Captures The Spirit

A great program name can serve as a connotation: an idea or feeling that a word/s invokes.

➥ *Friday Night Live* connotes TV's Saturday Night Live: It's the weekend! It's fun, live and unpredictable.

Brevity

The fewer words the better. Brief is good and easy: easy to remember, easy to print on promotional materials, easy to spell, easy to understand:

➥ *Reading 180* is designed to turn around students' reading ability 180 degrees.

➥ *Reading Is FUN-damental* sums up an elementary school reading program.

Clever And Creative

Often a great program name will have a double meaning or be a twist or a play on a common word or phrase, engaging the reader to think twice.

➥ *Strike A Chord* could be a name for a music program that goes beyond instruction and enthuses youth about the arts. The name has three connotations: 1) a peaceful, positive alternative for a group of violence-prone youth (i.e., "accord"), 2) it's what you do with an instrument, and 3) to "strike a chord" also means to spark someone's interest.

➥ *Walk N' Roll* is a program name to convey that a walk-a-thon to raise funds to supply wheelchairs to the indigent is going to have a different spin than the typical walk-a-thon.

➡ *Parents Count!* At first, this reads and sounds a lot like Character Counts!—and that's a plus. The program name is what parents will be doing with their children in this math program.

Active, Not Passive

The words in a great program name should suggest that the proposed program is positive and proactive:

➡ **CHANGES** (think the Tupac song) is a mentoring program designed to be a turning point for at-risk youth.

➡ *Project STOP* is a community collaborative formed to put an end to community violence.

➡ *Ready, Set, Gold!* combined the excitement of Los Angeles' Olympic bid with motivating children to set and reach their goals in the areas of fitness and health.

Reflects the Target Population

A great program name often mirrors the target population's ethnicity, language, culture, gender and/or age:

➡ *Adelante!* (meaning: "to move forward confidently") is a school-based counseling program for Hispanic youth.

➡ *Las Hermanas* ("the sisters") is a program where Latina businesswomen role model and mentor young, college-bound Latinas.

➡ *Give A Smile* is the name of a dental program
for indigent children in Mexico City and is also a
translation of a Mexican colloquialism.

Captures The Program's Comprehensiveness

Some great program names aptly describe the entire scope
of a program's services and goals:

➡ *Reading A–Z* covers all the basics of beginning
reading.

➡ *Six to Six* is a common name for extended school day
programs that provide programming for students from
as early as six in the morning to as late as six at night.

Followed By A Slogan

Again, using commercial advertising and marketing as
a model, a slogan (sometimes called a tag line) that follows
a program name should be just a few words, catchy, easily
remembered and explains the purpose of the program.

➡ *"10, 100, 1,000, 10,000"* could be a tag line for a
local jog-a-thon that tells the entire story: 10 will be
the total miles walked by 100 students who will earn
pledges of $10 per mile to achieve their goal of raising
$10,000 dollars.

➡ *Don't Be A Butthead* was an attention-getting tag
line that captured the non-smoking campaign aimed
at teenagers.

Logo A Go-Go

Whereas a program name captures the spirit of your program in words, a well-chosen symbol visually captures the spirit of your program. Wherever the program name goes, so should the logo—on every piece of material related to the program: correspondence, notebooks, banners, web sites, etc.

Acronym

Acronyms are words formed from the beginning letters of other words. Sometimes new words are formed and become part of the nomenclature. For example, Radar really stands for ra(dio) d(etection) a(nd) r(anging).

➤ *Project STOP* (Suppression Tactics & Opportunities for Prevention).

➤ **D.A.R.E.** (Drug Abuse Resistance Education).

There may be cases that your full program name is not as euphonious as the acronym that perfectly captures the spirit and mission of the program:

➤ *Lennox Invests In Fitness Education* is better known as **LIFE**.

➤ *Los Angeles's Better Educated Students For Tomorrow* is better known as **L.A.'s BEST.**

PITFALLS TO AVOID

Don't Use Your Agency's Name

This is number one on the hit parade of "pitfalls to avoid." It comes across too much like the self-aggrandizing name over the title in movies. You risk making the impression that promoting your agency is more important than promoting the purpose of the program.

Avoid A Sterile, Academic Program Name

"For All Intents And Purposes Emphatically Opine About The Inimical Ramifications Of Psychotropic Stupefacients!"

Try putting that one on a bumper sticker. Doesn't it read more like a graduate dissertation or a research experiment?

Said more simply: "Just Say No."

Whoops!

When you do come up with a program name, check for any possible acronyms that could be potentially embarrassing. Two examples:

➡ **CINCUS** (Commander in Chief, U.S. Fleet)
➡ **LSD High** The abbreviation for a proposed high school name.

Cutesy

And then there are some acronyms that are just too cutesy for their own good. While the example I am about to give is an actual program with an impeccable reputation and proven results helping parents provide educational enrichment for preschoolers nationwide, I personally can't believe how people can say the acronym with a straight face. Called *Home Instruction for Parents of Preschool Youngsters*, their program acronym is *HIPPY*. And it was started in the late sixties! Is it just me or does that acronym make it sound like school uniforms are hemp shirts and Earth Shoes with field trips taken to Grateful Dead concerts in a '68 VW bus?

THE PROCESS

1) **Be A Sponge:** We are a society of slogans, one-liners, taglines and brand names. Keep your eyes and ears open to what's around you: labels, billboards, packaging and other media. Talented people spend millions of hours and dollars researching and strategizing about how to get your attention. These effective, clever ideas will find you—otherwise they're not that clever or effective. So be a sponge and incorporate from them what works for your own program.

2) **Brainstorm:** That's "brainstorm" not "blame storm." This is where your Planning Team throws out any ideas no matter how far fetched. Keep in mind your program's Overarching Goal and your Target

Population. Don't judge, don't censor, don't qualify or rationalize, just come up with potential program names—good, bad and ugly.

3) **Relax, Have Fun:** Nothing stymies the creative process more than rules, rigidity, formality and negativity. So when the process feels forced, stop and figure out a way to create a playful environment and have some fun with it. Have contests with prizes for the best and worst possible name. Take turns listing as many possibilities, good, bad or ugly, in 30 seconds. Re-name movies and books. Stay positive. Just because you can't come up with a name doesn't mean you've failed. Often it's not a matter of creating a great program name, but instead, stumbling upon it.

4) **"Re-imagine" From Others:** Investigate other titles and program names to see if you can come up with a variation. Remember *Friday Night Live!?*

5) **Tap Into Other Sources:** Find phrases you can use from song titles, song lyrics, greeting cards, nursery rhymes, the Bible, Shakespeare, dictionaries, thesauruses or on-line idiom finders and acronym makers.

6) **Remember *Jon's Almost World Famous Seven Cs!*:** Often screenwriters stumped for a title will return to the basic fundamentals of their story to come up with

a title. For example, they may think of the clock in their story and embed it into the title (e.g., *48 Hours*). You can do the same with the Seven Cs of your program design. Review your Seven Cs and re-state each into a few words; it might spark the name of your program.

7) **Consult your Target Population:** See if they know of any proverbs, colloquialisms, idioms or phrases that capture the spirit and purpose of your program.

8) **Take the necessary time:** No matter how long it takes, no matter how loud the clock is ticking, no matter how rushed you are—take the time to come up with a great program name. Locking into a great program name also helps bring focus to your design and constantly reminds you—and the Reader/Scorer—about the Overarching Goal of your program.

9) **Legal issues:** After coming up with your program name, there is one more step. Either formally or informally find out if someone else is using the name. Usually, some individual or program already is. If you don't believe me, search "Walk N' Roll" on the Internet; a program name I was convinced no one had thought of before. The result? 2,070,000 hits. Ouch! So much for having an original thought. Others who have secured a trademark or service

mark often protect their program names from use. Although you can do the searching yourself informally (check the Internet, make calls, etc.), it is common to hire a law firm that specializes in conducting trademark searches and managing the application process, which, in the United States, can take up to six months. You may find that another program has the name you want but many miles separate your small program from theirs'. Often all it takes is a courtesy call to ask the program's permission to use the same name on a local basis for nonprofit purposes.

This process I propose for naming your program is nothing formal or set in stone. Chances are when you're following this suggested process you'll either invent a better method on your own or come up with a great program name before you reach the end.

Whatever works.

The point is, at some time during this process—and no one ever knows how, where, when or by whom—the program name will pop out and you'll look at each other and say, "That's it!" "It fits!" "Perfect!" "That's our program name!" This is usually followed by, "Why didn't we think of it four hours earlier???!!!!"

This all sounds good, right?

Makes sense, right?

Dude's talking from experience, right?

Wrong.

Easy advice to give but tough advice to follow.

As I write this, I'm working on a program design and for the life of me can't come up with a program name that fits all of the criteria above.

But, one must trust the process and follow her/his own advice. To prove this point I'm going to try an experiment. What I'm about to do is on the fly—nonstop—in one sitting—use the process and trust that I will come up with a program name.

No, not just any program name, a *great* program name!

MY PROCESS

So, as I trust the process, trust me when I say this is going to be one take – no stopping – unedited – just count the run on sentences and poor grammar. Here goes –

First, a little about the program.

We won a charter high school grant for a college-track academy that focuses on Mathematics, Science and Technology. Now we're applying for a grant to fund a specialized curriculum, basically a "school within a school."

Because the academy is located next to one of the world's largest airports, the focus is on aviation. The aviation-based program is designed to offer 9-12th grade students hands-on, aviation-themed, career exploration opportunities; new and advanced classes and special activities that prepare students for an aviation-related post-secondary education.

Unfortunately the best name I could come up with is the *Aviation Career Education Program*. The initials ACEP mean nothing. It's a lame program name.

Maybe ACE would work better but that's also a phrase associated with a fighter pilot. So, ACE gets, uh , shot down.

So, trust the process, I tell myself.

Here we go.

Step one. Brainstorm.

Flight - flight of fancy - Fly by - fly away - fly over - fly me to the moon

To the... something

Spread Your Wings - WINGS or WINGZ

Up to the....sky - up to the top over the top - at the top - top of the class - up in the air (oh, that's a great name that someone would want to fund) -

Stop censoring!!!

Aviation - sky - sky's the limit - don't want to use a limiting word like limit - sky so blue - blue skies

Back to fly - soar - SOAR!!!—implies to rise above Too good to be true - maybe make up an acronym - come up with words for each letter -

S = Students, sky, study, scholastic

O = options, optimal, over

A = academics, achievement,

R = ????

Okay, before I spend more time on trying
to work out an acronym, I'm going to search
SOAR on the Internet and see what's out there

[a few minutes later]

Wow – okay, not as original as I thought. But
I like the feeling of that one phrase, to rise
above –

Above – above, as in where the sky is – above,
as in head and shoulders – above all others –
above is what they'd be studying – above, as
in that thing above their shoulders is what
they're going to improve –

What about phrases that include "above?" –
go to the Internet and search idioms and
common phrases that include the above –

First, I'm going to go on iTunes to see if any
songs have above in it and look for phrases
that include "above." if nothing else I can
avoid work and listen to music for awhile ☺

Okay – here we go, iTunes power search results – above all – above all else – head above water – rise above – maybe there's something there – that goes on the possibility list "rise above, right under SOAR – the sky above – no, nothing else really – struck out there –

Thesaurus – Above: overhead, on/at the top, high up, on high, up above, (up) in the sky, high above one's head, aloft.

Aloft – elevated – raised – nothing there.

Back to the Internet and do a search of idioms and common phrases containing "above" – above board – above reproach –

WOW! Alert the media – start planning the ticker tape parade — I just got goosebumps – I found it, I swear – above and beyond

ABOVE AND BEYOND

Couple meanings there, the sky above and beyond all expectations, no limits – I LOVE it!!!!!!!!

Above and beyond is also associated with meritorious duty – as in, above and beyond the call of duty.

So the phrase "above and beyond" connotes: meritorious, beyond expectations, the sky's the limit, over and above – this one really works.

Search it on the Internet – few local uses, but it is a common phrase.

And copyright laws frown upon protection for short phrases. Their briefs state "... slogans, and other short phrases or expressions cannot be copyrighted." These short phrases are considered "common idioms" of the English language and are therefore, to use an idiom, "free to all."

As far as the phrase protected by trademark law? In this case, I believe this falls under "Service Marks" which refer to intangible activities which are performed by one person for the benefit of a person or persons other than himself, either for pay or otherwise. These issues are "above and beyond" my head and it's not my place in these pages to start discussing trademark law.

Can you say trademark lawyer?

But for the purposes of designing and applying for a grant, I say use the program name for submission purposes and explore the legalities once you've been awarded the grant.

But enough legalese.

The point is, "the process" was used to come up with a program name that works, that is marketable and sums up the program –

ABOVE AND BEYOND

Note: Please read the following in black and white, wearing a dark suit, while smoking. If possible, have your Planning Team in the background humming: "Doo-doo-doo-do, Doo-doo-doo-do..."

Witness if you will a funding agency executive entering an elevator. Just before the door is about to close another rider enters – but not just any rider. He is a prospective grantee from another dimension, a dimension of desperation.

He begins to make his pitch – a frantic pitch of never ending sight and sound.

The funding agency executive knows she is trapped.

She knows there is no way out.

She knows she has just entered...

THE HELLEVATOR ZONE.

Chapter 3-2

The Hell-evator Speech
OR, "I SHOULD HAVE TAKEN THE STAIRS"

Imagine you're a Director of a funding agency that writes checks to grantees for a living. You've been in the hotel ballroom offering advice to grantees all day. Or, you've just arrived at the hotel and checked in after a long flight and still have to prepare for tomorrow's workshop. Or, you're on your way up to your room hoping that you're not late for yet another conference call about, what else?, grants and programs.

You step into the elevator, you're tired, talked out, miss your family, your bladder's half-full (you're an optimistic funding executive) and you are actually looking forward to the brief respite of an elevator ride.

Then you're recognized. A grant writer begins reciting her/his polished, carefully calculated hell-evator speech that includes all the usual—type of program, target population, target area, proposed budget—designed to last until you reach your floor. Your first thought?

"I should have taken the stairs."

WHY HELL-EVATOR
SPEECHES DON'T WORK

No one likes to be spoon fed: What MOST grant writing books and self proclaimed gurus don't tell you is that no matter how unique, comprehensive, cutting edge and fundable your proposed program, when you boil it down like pabulum to a few sentences it can't help but sound a little derivative and a little vague. You can't possibly capture *all* the expertise and heart of your program in a polished, carefully calculated 60-second speech.

It's not the time or place: Whether it's in an elevator, waiting for a taxi, at a social event, during a break at a workshop or even at the next urinal over, no one wants to hear *all* about your program. Not there, not then.

It's too definitive: A polished, carefully calculated hell-evator speech is too conclusive and definitive. It allows the listener too much of an opportunity to jump to a conclusion about your program, without benefit of hearing the details. Your listener has to say no 100 times more than they say yes. And you've just given them an easy reason to say it.

You're telling them, not working *with* them: In many cases, these hell-evator speeches come across as inflexible, "we've made up or minds," take-it-or-leave-it propositions. An executive's quick way out is a polite "thanks but no thanks." Game over.

Feeding Frenzy On
The Funder Time

Someday, you will be in a situation where it's feeding frenzy on the funder time (that is, the ratio of those who want funding to those able to give it is about 100 to 1). Maybe a potential funder might happen to ask you "who are you with?" or "what are you working on?"

First, try acknowledging how busy they are, how generous they're being with their time, or how what they're saying makes sense.

Then, instead of the old Hell-evator speech, I propose you think of it as:

The "Little Bit Pregnant" Pitch

A little bit pregnant is a sales term meaning get the person "in bed with you", working with you, investing themselves in the idea, taking ownership, making it their own.

So the first step is to get the prospective funder to *not* say no, but instead get them to say something along the lines of:

"How do you propose to do that?"

"Can that be done?"

"Send me a few pages to remind me what we talked about."

So, LBP Rule #1 is to not sell them on your proposed program right there and then but instead get them eager to learn about the details later, at their convenience.

Work In Progress

When you do get the opportunity to describe your program, make sure that you describe it in a way that doesn't make it sound like it is set in concrete or "it's our way or the highway." Instead use phrases like:

"We're exploring a way to..." or,

"We've assembled some great thinkers who don't often work together to try to come up with a way to..." or,

"We're in the process of devising a new way to address the old problem of..."

From the potential funders point of view, this will allow your program to be shaped by and address the needs of their foundation (see "Ask Not What Your Funding Agency Can Do For You..." in the Bill Of Writes). They are the experts. They are also your prospective partner. They want to offer their expertise and support to see your idea come to fruition.

LBP Rule #2 is to frame your proposed program as a work in progress and position your team as being innovative and open to any support the potential funder/partner has to offer.

Know When To Shut Up

Your pitch should end when the potential funder lets you know what the next step will be. You're not there to describe the details of your program—only the basic concept. And only enough so they get it. If they want to hear more about your program they'll ask.

LBP Rule #3 paraphrases a quote often used in sales training: There is only one way to get anybody to do anything. And that is by making the other person want to do it.

Or, as Stan Laurel once said, "You can lead a horse to water but a pencil must be lead."

The One-Liner

I'm not implying that the idea of briefly synopsizing your proposed program should go the way of the dinosaur. There will be many occasions—a letter, publicity materials, brief applications, brochures—where you will need to summarize what is most unique about your proposed program in one sentence. For example, an effective one-liner for a non-profit might read:

> The Generic Mentoring Program is designed to reduce the high recidivism of gang-involved youth by using mentors who are from the law enforcement community.

A "LITTLE BIT PREGNANT" EXAMPLE

Now let's take ourselves to an imaginary Meet The Funders workshop where we are on a morning break after hearing a few foundation directors speak about —

Excuse me, but here comes a member of the panel looking for a cup of coffee.

"Thanks for the great tips," I say. "I liked what you had to say about the role of the lead agency."

"Good to hear that," she replies. "Who are you with?"

"The Generic Alternative High School in Blanksville," I say, "And I can't wait to get back and apply what I've learned here so far."

"So, what are you working on?" She asks while looking past me toward the path she'll take back to the dais.

For a split second I think: *Just say it, don't recite it. Know when to shut up:*

"Right now we're working on an entirely different approach to mentoring that involves at-risk juveniles in the court system getting a better understanding of the consequences of their crimes and law enforcement by talking with police officers in a mentoring situation."

She stops, looks at me for a moment, then after it sinks in: "Can you actually convince an officer to make peace with someone who may have threatened their life on the street just a few days before?"

I say, "That's what we thought at first, but we already have a Sheriff's sub-station on board and, because this is all new territory, we also involved a local mental health agency."

Now shut up, I think to myself.

"Very interesting," she says, "I'd like to know more about it when you have it all worked out."

"I'll do that," I say.

"Send me a letter, just a few pages. The guidelines are on our Website."

Too good to be true? It just doesn't happen that way, you think. Untrue. This kind of exchange has happened to me many times. Sometimes it's me (i.e., the one doing the pitching) who has to ask what the next step is (a meeting, a letter, a proposal), but it's always a result of the impetus of the potential funder.

One key ingredient missing from the above? A clever and compelling name for the program, as discussed in the previous chapter.

Second, make sure whoever is representing your program is enthusiastic, an expert, prepared and persuasive.

Third, make sure the pitch is rehearsed, refined, tried out on a wide range of listeners, then refined and rehearsed some more. As actors say, rehearse it until it doesn't sound rehearsed.

✢   ✢   ✢

Try this process of paring down your program design into a LBP pitch. Not only will it prepare you for that chance encounter with a potential funder, it will also help spotlight your program's unique selling points that stand out from others'.

Chapter 3-3

Researching Grants
SHOW ME THE GRANT MONEY!

"Oh, you're like that guy..."

Whenever people find out I have something to do with helping nonprofits design viable programs and writing grants to fund their cause, they immediately think of:

"... that crazy guy on TV who says there's millions of dollars of grant money out there just waiting..."

Actually, there are several guys like that: wearing wardrobes that even Batman's arch enemies wouldn't wear; standing in front of some federal-government-looking building with fistfuls of dollars; barking at us like carnival sidemen about the loads of grant money out there to do whatever we want: "write a novel, travel, eat out at a different restaurant every night, get paid for sleeping!" And all we have to do is send them one hundred bucks for a catalog—yeah, a catalog that we can get for free from the federal government.

Many grant seekers are drawn to applying for grants because of a similar ideal: there's a mountain of grant money hidden out there waiting for the first non-profit to stumble upon it.

I'm sure many of you have heard of fill-in-the-blank letters written to a foundation or a corporation and, a few weeks later, a check is delivered with four zeros in it.

My services and advice are often sought out by those who "want to know how to write one of *those* letters" to help themselves, or their program get-rich-quick. Within the past month I received a call from someone who wanted to find the money that's out there to fund her five-month hiking tour of Europe. And, oh yeah, she was leaving in three weeks.

Did she really think that if I knew of a way to subsidize a five-month hiking tour of Europe that I'd be sitting here in my office?

Unfortunately, as with the program design process, there are no shortcuts to seeking out and applying for funding sources. Even in the competition for the smallest grant awards, a tremendous amount of forethought, time and effort need to be invested in the process.

As for those who want to get rich the quickest? They also are the ones who give up their pursuit the quickest.

By the way, I suspect the hiker in Europe found her mountain of money—through her Mom and Dad.

Researching funding sources should NOT be something done when you realize your program is running out of money, because the rent is due in three weeks or you need grant funds as some sort of financial band-aid.

Your team is not a programmatic crisis intervention team; they are a *Planning* Team.

In this chapter I'm going to outline a way to help you make grant researching an on-going process and an integral part of your operations.

FIRST THINGS FIRST

Researching funding sources should be part of an on-going, year-round systematic plan. Much like you would include a line item in your agency budget to ensure that there's money on hand when you need it for a certain component of program delivery, searching and researching should be budgeted into your agency or program's time schedule and staff job responsibilities.

The benefits will not be immediate, but they will payoff in the long term if you have—

A Point Person

Do not confuse this position with the one in your agency or program who is in charge of fundraising and charity events, or soliciting personal donations. This point person's sole responsibility should be tracking, and applying for, grant funding opportunities. Time and resources should be allotted for this person to participate in on-going training, workshops and any activities that will give them "face time" with grant makers.

A Development Notebook

One responsibility of the point person should be to keep a regularly updated development notebook that includes: hard copies of current leads or tips for new funding sources; contact info logs (who was contacted, when and for what reason); a status report of submitted proposals; a yearly calendar of deadlines, upcoming workshops and bidders conferences; copies of related correspondence; and a brief history of grants awarded the agency or program. Updates to, and discussions about, this development notebook should become a permanent agenda item of your regular staff meetings.

This information should be so organized and self-explanatory that, in the point person's absence, anyone in your program or on your Planning Team could pick it up and continue the work without missing a beat.

A Willingness To Start Smaller

While, at first, you may have grand dreams for a more comprehensive, bigger budgeted program, it's important to remember that less of a budget means, from the funding agency's point-of-view, less of a risk.

Just because you may be a smaller agency or a program with less of a track record, you are not at a disadvantage; that is, if you think in terms of initially implementing a scaled-down version of your program with a scaled-down budget.

And here's the biggest advantage of this "start smaller" philosophy. When you request more funds for a larger project, you will be requesting funds to expand your *existing* program that has *documented success over a period of years.* Further, it will have been operated by an organization in which the funding agency has confidence. In this case, your track record will give you the inside track.

Remember The Bill Of Writes

Revisit "Ask Not What The RFP Can Do For You, But What You Can Do For the RFP." MOST grant writers err by trying to fit the funding agency's RFP to their pre-existing program plan design rather than designing a program to address the specific grant requirements.

Do Your Homework

It's not necessary to have every detail of your program worked out but, throughout this research process, you'll need to know the basics of your program. *Jon's Almost World Famous Seven Cs!* and developing your Little Bit Pregnant Pitch will provide you with those.

TYPES OF GRANTS

Your proposal will be submitted to, and your money is going to come from, one of four funding sources:

Federal Grants

For every federal agency or program, it seems like each generates grants as well. Federal grants usually have the biggest budgets, span the longest period of time (some up to six years), are the most competitive (you're competing with programs/agencies from all 50 states) and are the most complex in terms of forms, budgets, narrative response requirements, program monitoring, and evaluation.

Although federal grants are awarded to programs of all sizes and budgets, the feds have a tendency to fund larger, more stable, established, financially solvent, non-profit collaboratives (there's that word "collaborative" again) with an exemplary track record.

Federal proposals are rigorously evaluated and scored based on a pre-determined set of standards. This makes the competition more anonymous and is meant to set-up a "may the best application with the highest score win" situation. Often, to prevent any potential bias by readers, the proposals are read with the name and location of the agency crossed out.

The feds are notorious for strictly enforcing their rejection criteria. For example, I know of one perfectly good federal application that was disqualified due to signatures signed in black, not blue, ink.

State Grants

State grants might be generated by various state departments (e.g., education, human services, criminal justice) or they might be federal funds funneled through a state agency. While state grants may be a little less complicated than federal grants, make no mistake, they are still incredibly complex. Like the feds, state grants tend to offer long-term funding (most average three years).

Regional/County Grants

These local grants are usually distributed on a county- or city-wide basis, meaning your lead agency must be headquartered in those areas. Generally awarded for a shorter period of time (one or two years), these grants award less money than state or federal grants. The application requirements of both city and county grants are far less complicated than state and federal grants. Also, these funding agency staff are more apt to work with, and fund, smaller, upstart non-profit entities.

Foundation Grants

Foundation grants are those that come from corporations, individual philanthropists, community/private foundations or trust funds. Like local grants, these are generally for lesser amounts, a shorter period of time (one or two years) and have a far less complicated application process than state and federal grants. Often, only a two to four-page letter is required.

A key to winning foundation grants is establishing a relationship with an officer or executive from the foundation.

While local and foundation funding sources may be less stringent, the application process is often more political. Political meaning, often but not always, a grant award is based on a relationship between one of your staff or team and a program officer at the foundation.

INVITATIONS TO APPLY

Funding sources invite potential applicants to apply for their funds in three forms:

Request for Proposals (RFP)

Got a wheelbarrow?

An RFP is usually a thick packet that includes extensive discussion and research findings of the problems to be addressed, the funding agency's mission, specific questions to address in the response and all required forms to be completed. It also includes deadlines and due dates, other application requirements, dos and don'ts, announcements for conferences and workshops to assist applicants, links to resources to study the problem or existing funded programs addressing the problems. These RFPs often include the text of the legislation that authorized the funding.

Request for Applications (RFA) or Request For Funding (RFF)

An RFA/RFF is all the above but is usually sent out to a program or agency as an invitation for reapplication or an extension of funding to programs/agencies who already have a grant. Or, these can be sent to a group of pre-selected potential grantees who have been screened by the funding agency and then invited to submit a proposal.

Letters of Inquiry (LOI)

Usually requested by local and foundation grant sources, LOIs are designed to prevent the applicant from doing a lot of unnecessary work. They also reduce unnecessary reading for the funding agency staff.

LOIs are one to three page letters that briefly identify the problem to be addressed, who's addressing it, how it's going to be addressed, the request for support, how long it will take and the changes (or outcomes) that will occur. Agency staff will screen these very brief and succinct letters and invite those applicants who qualify to submit a more detailed proposal. As simple as it may first appear, *an LOI is a lot of work.* Writing an LOI can sometimes feel as challenging as turning a 60-page federal response into a 17-syllable Haiku poem. LOIs need to be written in a very straightforward and specialized way.

WHERE TO LOOK

Web Sites

Most funding agencies—or in the case of government grants, their sponsoring agencies—have a Web site. These Web sites have links labeled something like "New Funding Opportunities" or "Grant Announcements." Once you find an appropriate site, bookmark it so you can check in every month as part of your search and research process. In many cases, provide your e-mail address and these sites will imme-diately alert you about any new grant opportunities.

www.grants.gov

In 2002, www.grants.gov was established as a governmental resource named the E-Grants Initiative. Grants.gov is a cen-tral storehouse for information on over 1,000 grant programs and access to approximately $400 billion in annual awards. By registering once on this site, your organization can apply for, and manage, grants from the 26 federal grant-making agencies. You do not have to register with Grants.gov if you only want to find grant opportunities. If you do plan to apply for a grant, be aware that you and your organization must complete the Grants.gov registration process which can take up to two weeks—and that's if all steps are completed on a timely basis. So register early! Also, sign up for the "Succeed" Newsletter, a guide to the latest updates, handy tips and useful articles on how to best use Grants.gov.

ListServs

Many non-profit assistance centers, foundations and even private grant writing firms will do a lot of this research work and invite you to be on the list of those who wish to be e-mailed when new funding opportunities are announced.

However, many private grant writing firms will also make you weed through a lot of "why-you-should-hire-us-to-write-your-grant-instead-of-doing-it-yourself" come ons. After bypassing the hype, the information is usually accurate and helpful.

How do you find ListServs? Search "grant writing," "grant funding," "grant opportunities," etc. on the Internet and you'll be busy for a few days. The benefit of these lists is that they compile smaller, lesser-known regional grants (along with the bigger ones) that you might overlook in your own search.

Foundation Centers

Established in 1956, and supported by more than 600 foundations from across the nation, the New York-based Foundation Center (www.foundationcenter.org) is the nation's leading authority on philanthropy, connecting nonprofits and the grant makers supporting them. It also operates research, education, and training programs designed to advance philanthropy at every level. The Center's web site receives more than 47,000 visits each day. Thousands of people access free resources in its five regional library/learning centers and its national network of more than 340 cooperating collections. Their user-friendly web site is designed to guide you quickly to the information you are looking for—instruction on funding research, help with proposal writing, tools for locating prospective funders, news and research on the field, or a nearby foundation, library or training class. Through the web site, you can access over 90,000 foundations and corporate donors. Their user interface, as simple as searching for a book in a library, has 36 specific search fields. Foundation subject categories include grant types, funders by state, grants by amounts, grants in categories, profiles of funders, grants by deadline, etc. These guides can also be found as books or

CD-ROMs, often at your local library, but they are usually outdated.

On the west coast, the Emerald City for nonprofits is The Center for Nonprofit Management. In addition to providing many of the same services as its New York counterpart, the Center has an outstanding reputation for developing nonprofit leadership and management skills and promoting collaboration and communication between nonprofits.

Community Foundations

These are non-profit agencies established to act as superintendents of trust funds and donations by local philanthropists whose mission is to give back to and support the local community. These foundations educate and empower local non-profit groups and agencies to start-up, operate and sustain various programs. These foundations can also serve as a hub to help your program staff network with other agencies, programs, resources and funding sources in your area. Community foundations often have a reference library of research resources and they host various workshops.

Staff there have great insight into who is giving out money and for what purposes. These foundations often archive all their activities so if you happen to miss something important, you can go there later and watch a video or read a transcript of the session you missed.

Becoming a familiar face at, and get on the mailing list of, the nearest community foundation in your area is absolutely essential.

Meet The Grantor Sessions

Usually conducted by foundations, these local workshops offer the opportunity for you the potential grantee to meet, hob nob, ask questions of—but not shamelessly beg—staff and officers representing various local and national foundations. Just remember to prepare your Little Bit Pregnant Pitch and one-line concept.

These meetings should be put on your organization's "must attend" list and are extremely critical to you getting an edge over your competitors.

Grant Writing Workshops

These half-day, day-long, multi-day or multi-week sessions are offered by local foundations, community colleges or for-profit grant-writing businesses.

Frankly, I'm not a big fan of 4–8 hour sessions. I find them useful as an introduction to the process and the possibilities, but little help when it comes to the step-by-step process of designing and writing a grant. Usually, agency staff and grant writers leave these workshops all fired up and ready to go. That is, until they face the reality of the blank page and then they're back to where they were—not having a real process to design and write a winning grant.

If you should decide to attend a workshop, seek out a class that puts as much, or more, emphasis on "getting it right before you write"—that is, the design and structure of a program, instead of phrasing responses and filling out forms. It should be a class that is long enough in duration to take students through each step of the process and give them weekly feedback on their project as they progress.

➡ *Note:* Beware of for-profit classes offered by a grant writing firm where they seem more intent on making the process convoluted and overwhelming. They're trying to get you to throw your hands in the air so you hire them (usually at an exorbitant cost) to do it all for you.

Local Libraries

Usually, the friendly reference desk staff at your local library can point you to a shelf, alcove or a handful of books that might provide some helpful materials. For example, in the area I live, a library 20 miles from here has what amounts to a satellite office of a county foundation located right inside the library. The library in town here also has a shelf full of how-to books for non-profit agencies. Just watch out though, some of their sources are too outdated.

Other Non-Profit Agencies And Programs In Your Area

You might be surprised to know that most non-profit agencies will be more than happy to share knowledge, contacts, information about grants and grant-givers with other non-profits—okay, maybe not the ones you'll be in direct competition with, but most.

Staff from these agencies can be an especially valuable resource if they've won a grant from the funding agency you are applying to. How do you find these groups? Keep an eye on your local newspaper for coverage and announcements of their activities. Chances are you cross paths with them at various functions throughout the year. Beyond that, funding agency web sites often maintain a list of programs and groups that they currently fund in your area. Don't hesitate to approach these local winners of grants for information. In most cases, part of the requirement for fulfilling their grants is to disseminate information about their program.

Grant Writers/Firms Who Will Conduct Your Search For A Fee

This is an option, but not one I recommend. First, it's relatively expensive and, in my mind, you are better off putting that research money toward program design and the writing of the grant. Second, ferreting out future funding sources should become part of your daily operations so that your program becomes self-sustaining. Third, applying the principles of this book's third section will prepare you to do what you would have hired one of these firms to do.

Now that you know what's out there and where to find it, the next step is to play matchmaker. But first, there's a little matter to resolve involving a chicken and an egg.

Chapter 3-4

Compatibility
DEEP AND IMPORTANT I$$UE$

Alert the media—the age-old "What-came-first-the-chicken-or-the-egg?" philosophical puzzle was definitively unscrambled by university researchers who recently released this scientific finding:

> A chicken and an egg are lying on a bed. The egg is smoking a cigarette with a satisfied smile on its face and the chicken is frowning and looking quite miffed.
>
> The egg mutters, "Well, I guess we answered THAT question!"

And that's their final answer.

However, program design still has the same sort of unanswered circular question: What should come first? Do you design your best program then search for a potential funding agency? Or, do you find potential funding sources and then come up with a program skewed to what those funding agencies are funding at the time?

I say design your program first—but that's not quite my final answer.

By "design your program first" I mean use *Jon's Almost World Famous Seven Cs!* to design a program that targets your Planning Team's unique expertise and experience at your Target Population's unique and critical needs. This combination will ensure that your program will be seriously considered for funding and one that your collaborative can implement and manage.

Now here's my final answer—*don't stop there.*

Instead, align your initial program design with the strategy from the Bill Of Writes: "Ask Not What The RFP Can Do For You, Ask What You Can Do For the RFP."

Alignment is the key.

Find a funding agency that funds programs in the area of the program you propose. Then, after familiarizing yourself with the specifics of that funding agency's program plan, mission and outcomes, re-tool your initial program design to specifically align with that funding agency's specific program plan, mission and outcomes.

In Over Their Programmatic Heads

Personally, I avoid working with programs or agencies whose practice is to go willy-nilly after any and all monies out there. Too often they find themselves in over their programmatic heads. In their desperate attempts to acquire funds to keep their sinking program afloat, they posture as experts in an area—any area where funds are available—then fall short when it comes to delivering the services promised. Sure, this hurts their reputation and jeopardizes their chances of receiving other grants.

But, more importantly, it hurts the populations they fail to serve.

For example, a funding agency announces that they are releasing funds to address the critical needs of inner-city latchkey upper grade elementary students who are home alone during the high crime times of 3–6 p.m. A desperate or unethical preschool program may rationalize that "kids are kids are kids" and, with their program desperate for money (bills are bills are bills), may portray themselves as qualified to be caretakers of children. In truth, their staff is trained only as experts for 3–4 year olds, not 10–12 year olds. If the unethical program should happen to receive an award, they would not have the facilities, the training, the expertise or the experience to work with the older student population.

On the other hand, an ethical program—let's use a senior center for an example—may learn of the grant competition described above. First, this ethical senior program would create a planning team of experts to design a specific program that would help the disadvantaged teens *and* seniors at the center. This could involve hiring and training those teens to help out with assisting the seniors. In turn, the teens would make some money, stay out of trouble, learn empathy, acquire workplace skills and reap the benefits of community service. The ethical planning team would make sure that all activities are *within the expertise* of those involved and that they also align with the funding agency's program plan, mission and outcomes.

My Final Answer

So, back to the question: Which should come first, the program or the funding source?

I say the most ethical, efficient and beneficial thing to do is first design a program that best uses the expertise of your Planning Team to serve the unaddressed critical needs of the disadvantaged populations you serve. Then, find a funding agency with the same program plan, mission and outcomes.

And, that's *my* final answer.

Finding The Right Funding Agency: The First Three Steps

In trying to find a potential funding agency, you're looking for—as they say at the online dating services—more than surface compatibility. You're looking for the deep and important issues that truly matter in a serious, long-term relationship.

Of course, a big, fat check that will keep your program afloat for three years wouldn't be so bad either.

Using the previous chapter as a guide, you narrowed down a list of funding agencies offering grants aligned with your program design. Now save your Planning Team time by narrowing down that list even more. To do this, verify that you are eligible for, and will be competitive to win, the grant according to the requirements of each potential funding agency.

First, revisit the "Get Out of Writing Free" chapter of this book. That chapter pinpoints reasons why you shouldn't even bother applying or launching into a program design.

Second, carefully read the *most recent* Program Solicitation or Announcement guidelines in each RFP or grant announcement. Each program's solicitation specifies requirements for that program and crucial information Reader/Scorers will use to review the proposal. This review criteria is particularly important to consider in your decision to pursue the grant.

Third, make sure that you contact or visit the web site of the funding agency for any updates to these guidelines or program solicitations. Also look for any responses to Frequently Asked Questions (FAQs) and archived versions of Web casts or PowerPoints about their funding opportunities.

Fourth, if a member of your Planning Team knows staff of a program or agency who has received a grant from the funding agency, then pick their brain for insight into that funding agency's preferences.

Finding The Right Funding Agency: Eligibility Questions

➤ How do you like them odds?

Assuming your grant application will be complete enough for serious consideration, what are the odds of your team winning?

Do the math.

But let's not use the word odds. "Odds" implies that it's a total crapshoot.

And, it's only a crapshoot if you write crap.

Instead, let's use the term mathematical probability. Using mathematical probability, work off the assumption that there will be more equally qualified applicants than there will be grants awarded.

But the question is, do you have enough of a chance at winning to make it worth your Planning Team's while to apply? The answer lies in the total amount of awards the funding agency plans to dole out and the average amount of each award.

For example, if a federal agency announces that they are releasing a total of $8.5 million dollars in grant funds divvied up into awards averaging $1.7 million dollars each over a two-year period, then that means only five grants will be awarded nationwide ($8,500,000/ $1,700,000 = 5 awards).

Considering that some federal grants attract 500+ applications, I don't like the probability of winning the above grant. First, it's too long of a long shot. Second, you may be a smaller program in a smaller community—and that grant amount would be more than triple the amount of your operating budget. That total is obviously for a larger program in a larger city or spread out over a larger region.

On the other hand, if $90 million dollars in 21st Century Learning grants are released and the announcement suggests that each grantor will receive approximately one million dollars over five years, then that translates as a minimum of 90 grant awards ($90,000,000/$1,000,000 = 90 awards).

Despite the fact there may be over 400 applicants, I like those chances better. Remember this is the grant writing business; even the best chances will seem nearly impossible.

Indiana Jones is famous for the line, "Never tell me the odds." As the self-proclaimed Indiana Jones of grant writers, I prefer, "Never tell me the odds—until after I beat them."

Another factor is geographic distribution of funds. If part of the funding agency's decision is equitably doling out funds throughout all portions of an entire geographic region, then that may worsen your odds. For example, a few years ago in California, an RFP was issued for community-based health clinic funds. I was approached by a smaller community on the fringe of the greater L.A. metro area about designing a program for them. Only five grants were being awarded throughout the state.

Buried in that RFP somewhere was a statement like:

> "...decisions for funding will be based on the highest scores [*I liked that*]...the greatest need [*we could have easily argued that*]...and will be equitably distributed throughout five regions in the state [*curses, spoiled again*]."

Five grants for five regions throughout the entire state of California—*and Southern California was considered one region!* Southern California includes the major metro areas of San Diego, Los Angeles and Orange County. One grant for the entire area and, because I did my homework and researched the past awards issued by the funding agency, they had a tendency to award grants to inner-city programs. No thanks.

➤ Does Your Organization/Lead Agency Fulfill The Non-Profit Status Requirements Of The Funding Agency?

Research each potential funding agency's *current* definition and requirements for non-profits. Don't rely on what someone else tells you. And don't rely on a general belief that "all those requirements are basically the same."

Some funding agencies only require formal proof of your organization having been a non-profit agency for a minimum of one year. Others require that you have been in operation for up to three years.

Are you or your fiscal agency/sponsor a tax-exempt charitable organization? If so, they may ask that you include a copy of your 501(c)(3) Determination Letter.

Or, are you a governmental tax-exempt unit? If so, include verification. Private organizations must generally have valid tax exemption status under Section 501(c)(3) of the IRS Code and be classified as a public charity and not as a "private foundation" under Section 509(a)(1).

Is your agency in the process of applying for non-profit status? Unfortunately, most funding agencies will look at your organization as undesirable because you have no track record.

This is for three reasons: 1) most start-ups fold soon after they are established, 2) a start-up has little experience operating a program, and 3) there are many unscrupulous types who form fly-by-night non-profits in an attempt to get quick cash—from individuals, philanthropists and foundations.

Also look at the requirements for the lead agency. Some funding agencies require that it be one specific type of organization (e.g., a school district). Others require that a lead agency serve a minimum number of clients, have a certain size budget or have a minimum number of full-time staff.

➤ Does Your Organization Fulfill The Audit History Requirements Of The Funding Agency?

This one catches many program and agency staff off guard. Some funding agencies require that you not only include audits from your past three years of operations but also that these audits be conducted by a licensed external auditor. Others require that you only submit your latest audit, as long as it was completed within the past three years.

➤ Does Your Organization Fulfill The Financial Requirements Of The Funding Agency And Do You Have Documented Proof Of Those Requirements?

Funding agencies may require up to four forms of proof:

- Your most recent profit and loss statement.
- Your current year's budget with year-to-date financial figures.

- If applicable, a copy of your most current IRS Form 990 including Schedule A.
- Proof of financial solvency. One state grant, for example, wanted applicants to show proof that:

"...the applicant agency possesses sufficient fiscal resources to start up and operate the program being requested for a period of UP TO THREE MONTHS (90 days of operation) without any payments from the state."

> ➤ **Can You Provide The Cash Or In-Kind Matches Required By The Funding Agency?**

Verify the amount of money/resources that the funding agency requires your collaborative to contribute toward the proposed program. This will be in the form of either a cash match or in-kind, donated services or labor. As discussed in the Collaboration chapter, in-kind is usually not a problem. However, the cash match requirement could be. The required amount of the cash-match can vary from as little as 10% to as much as dollar-for-dollar.

Personally, I shy away from the dollar-for-dollar cash match ditties. That means, on a $100,000 grant, for example, your collaborative would have to come up with a $100,000 cash match. It feels like too much of an "all in" bet in Texas Hold 'Em. Besides, if your group had those kinds of resources laying around, would you really be looking for grants?

➤ Are There Any Geographic Restrictions On The Grant Award?

Geographic restrictions vary. Some funding agencies only allocate grant funds to programs serving certain clients living only within a specific geographic zone. Or, these restrictions might prohibit program operations to extend beyond a state or county line. Also, there are often geographic mandates about where your program needs to be headquartered. For example, your lead agency might need to be physically located within the same zip code as those to which they provide services. This is the funding agency's way of ensuring that programs and program staff have roots in the community.

➤ Do You Know All The Deadlines And Timeline Requirements, And Can You *Realistically* Meet Them?

Federal, state and most local grants make this one VERY clear—specifying the exact date and exact time that the proposal needs to be submitted. In most cases they'll even specify whether the grant has to be *in their office* by the deadline or *postmarked* by the deadline.

If you are required to submit a grant application on-line, be warned that this method is FAR from perfect. Often, you'll encounter a slew of crashes, delays and complications for which the funding agency will take no responsibility. The only way to avoid this is to file early.

But don't think in terms of submission dates only. Often the funding agency will specify when they want winning programs to be up and running and fully operational. There was one case where a funding agency released an RFP in early spring with a submission deadline of late May. Grants were awarded in mid-June and they wanted programs operational by the beginning of September— *less than three months after award notification!* Even if you're a huge, experienced agency that's hard to do. But if you're a smaller, start-up agency make sure you know what you're getting into as far as timeline requirements.

Foundations with open submission dates or year-round submissions are trickier. While their stated policy may be to *accept* applications and LOIs year-round, they often only *consider* them at certain times of the year. If those times of the year are not specified, then the key to knowing when they consider applications are their Board of Director meetings. This is because, while foundation staff may screen and recommend proposals for funding, it's usually the Board that has the final say. And some boards may meet only three times a year (usually early fall, soon after the New Year, in the spring—but hardly ever in the summer). So, for example, if you are requesting funds for a summer camp that begins right after school gets out in June—you want to make sure your application gets through to the board at its January meeting, not when it meets in June.

The best thing to do here is pick up the phone and ask one of the staff at the foundation. Their first response will usually be a well rehearsed, "we accept submissions year-round." However, if you follow up with an, "Okay, but for a program that we want to start in the fall when would be the *most appropriate time* to submit an application?" they will get the idea that you know what you're talking about and they'll provide a better, more specific time. At the least, they could tell you when their board is scheduled to meet.

> ➤ **Are You Prepared To Meet The Reporting And Evaluation Requirements Of The Funding Agency?**

More and more funding agencies now require that you spend a percentage (sometimes up to 20%) of your budget on a professional evaluation component. They may require that a collaborative partner have advanced experience in this area of evaluation or that you partner with a local college or university—or a professional evaluation firm—as part of a larger evaluation plan. Other agencies may require that you establish a system of record keeping and reporting that could overburden your program or require additional staff that you cannot afford to hire. Know the legal, financial and logistical requirements of reporting and evaluation—and verify that you can fulfill them—*before* you begin your application process.

> ➤ **If Applying For A Foundation Grant, Are You Requesting Support From A Person And Not Just A Place?**

Joan Rivers once joked about business that, "It's not WHO you know, it's WHOM."

That no one I know has ever laughed at that great line is not important.

What is important is—like it or not—with foundation, local and some state grants—whom you know, with whom you've built relationships, and whom you've schmoozed on the funding side plays a key role in the grant-making process. This is especially true because local foundation staff are more apt to answer a question over the phone or, in a very basic way, help an applicant tailor their response for their upcoming grant award process, if they have established a relationship with that person. These staff also know members of foundation and funding agency boards and their likes and dislikes.

The test for this question lies in your cover letter or Letter Of Inquiry. Is your salutation addressed to a specific person (that's excellent) or is it addressed as MOST applicant do, to a group or generic job title (e.g., "Dear Selection Committee).

➤ You May Know What The Agency Funds, But Do You Know What It *Doesn't* Fund?

Most funding agencies, no matter the size of the grants they award, will specify what they absolutely will not fund. So before you spend a lot of time and effort, double-check this section of the grant guidelines. This may be listed as "Types Of Programs (or Line-Items) Not Funded." If the information is not in the grant guidelines, then look on the agency's web site.

Here are some examples of what some funding agencies may not consider: on-going operating costs, faith-based services, human experimentation, purchase of vehicles, educational videos, documentaries, and the list goes on and on. If you're unsure, contact a funding agency representative directly. Just make sure and have your Little Bit Pregnant Pitch ready so you don't waste their time.

> ➤ **Are You Aware Of The Funding Agency's Currently Funded Projects And Programs?**

Most funding agency Web sites will either have links to, or a downloadable PDF about, programs they have funded. Information will include where these funded programs are located, how much was awarded, for what length, a description of the program and some of their successes.

Why is it important to know this? First, you don't want to submit a proposed program that duplicates existing services in your area. Second, this knowledge will give you an idea of how much the funding agency allocates per certain type of program. Third, you can learn specifics about programs they do fund and use some of those components in your own program design.

A good example of this recently occurred when a planning team explored the web site of a large California foundation whose efforts were geared toward the "…emotional, educational and healthful development of children ages six months to three years old." We had pretty much decided on a particular daycare curriculum until we explored their web site; specifically, recently funded programs like ours. We found a common component that made us completely change our approach. The programs they funded all involved parent education, literacy and empowerment much more than ours. So while the grant said that they targeted *children* ages up to three years-old, what they were really interested in were children *and their families.* That changed our approach to the program (i.e., we focused more on parents becoming full partners in the process) and the budget.

There's one other good reason to do this preliminary research. If in a conversation with funding agency staff, or in an LOI written to them, you are able to reference examples of what their agency has funded, and/or are currently funding, that will demonstrate that you have done your homework, are professional and not using a scattergun approach in a desperate attempt to get funding.

From a funding agency's perspective, those who use a scattergun approach are nothing more than scatterbrains.

✛ ✛ ✛

Now that you've narrowed your sights on a few funding agencies and are sure that your program and the funding agency are compatible, it's time to take another look at the RFP—this time with an eye toward winning a grant.

Chapter 3-5

Reading The RFP
THE BETTER THE READER,
THE BETTER THE WRITER

You think, "RFP might as well stand for Redundant, Frustrating and Piddling."

Or you may think, "I already know how to read an RFP, start on page one and go from left to right."

Or, "Reading the RFP? Please. If there's any chapter worth skipping in this book ..."

But stop and think about this: if the reason you're reading this book is that you keep applying for grants and are getting the same negative results as MOST applicants, then maybe what you're thinking right now might be the problem.

Or, I should say, *how* you're thinking right now might be the problem.

If you refuse to do whatever is necessary to make your programs more competitive—including reading and re-reading an RFP because you consider it to be "...redundant, frustrating and piddling..."— how do you expect to be chosen over your competitors who *will* do the necessary extra work?

So, if you're still with me, this chapter is about reading with a new set of eyes that will enable you to: (1) decipher and read between the lines of the RFP, (2) ensure that your program design aligns with the intent of the RFP, and (3) extract unanswered questions and buried requirements that need clarification in the RFP.

Of the applicants I know who aren't winning as many grants as they would like to:

MOST plan as well as others.

MOST write as well —if not better—than others.

But MOST have one big deficiency.

MOST don't *read* RFPs and application materials as well as their more successful peers.

Reading An RFP
Can Be Frustrating

First, an RFP is very technical and dry and not something you'd take to the beach in the summer—unless you intend to fall asleep and get badly sunburned.

Second, RFPs are often unclear and contradictory because of how they are written or, more accurately, how they are *not written*. Seldom does one wordsmith with one vision, one voice and an abundance of uncluttered time, write an RFP. Instead, an RFP as a result of last-minute political compromise, might be hurriedly patched together by committee. Bits and pieces of irrelevant languages and requirements are cut and pasted from previous grants. Legal passages are excerpted from legislation. Outdated forms are incorporated from other programs that might not exactly match the needs and language of your particular project.

In other cases, the RFP may blatantly contradict itself. Or, some RFPs state the same piece of information in an ever-so-slightly different way in different places.

Personally, I understand how and why all this happens. Does this make it any easier on your Planning Team trying to unscramble the RFP? No. So just getting through it is the first step—and the biggest one.

Back In The Highlight Again

One of the best investments you can make is a set of highlighters in five or six different colors.

Then, read the RFP through several times focusing on one particular aspect. Each time you come across something having to do with that aspect color-code it with a highlighter.

For example, your yellow highlighter may be used for all budgetary matters. A blue highlighter might separate all matters relating to programmatic components (e.g., staffing ratios, number of clients served, etc.) A green highlighter might flag submission requirements of the RFP (e.g., letters of support, attachments, forms). A pink highlighter (am I running out of colors yet?) could be used to highlight those elements that will require further discussion by your Planning Team.

This highlighter method: (1) will help you learn the RFP backwards and forwards by reading it many, many times; (2) better organize your response; (3) provide you with a ready checklist of "to dos;" and (4) help you find sections of the RFP fast when it matters most, during brain crunching, last-minute deadlines. Eventually, you won't need highlighters. Your brain will become trained to sort, organize and make lists from the RFP.

Another suggestion that has made my life easier is to also use Post-Its™ to flag each section of the RFP so you can quickly flip to those relevant sections.

All of this is not a waste of time or unnecessary work. By organizing the RFP you're organizing your thoughts and making yourself a better reader.

And the better the reader, the better the writer.

Ask Not What Your RFP Can Do For You, But What You Can Do For Your RFP

I'll say it again: this is a vital concept (as explained in the Bill of Writes) that 99% of those new to program design don't understand—nor do 98% with some experience. It's also the key concept that is the difference between winning and losing a grant.

MOST applicants try to fit the funding agency's RFP to their pre-existing program design, rather than modifying their program design to address the mission of the funding agency and the RFP.

So, put on the brakes—pause here for a moment—and really understand this concept. Inventory the past few grants you've submitted and see if the term MOST applicants applies to you, even by just a tiny bit.

And then remember in any competition MOST applicants lose, by just a tiny bit.

So, how do you *not* repeat the mistakes made by MOST applicants?

In One Word: Alignment

Your program plan, mission and outcomes should align with the funding agency's plan, mission and outcomes. In this example taken from an actual school violence reduction RFP that's on my desk as I write this, there is a line that mentions:

> "...while the funding agency will consider all types of programs, those whose services are more proactive than reactive will be deemed more in line with the department's overall vision..."

Anybody got a decoder ring?

First, go to their web site and find the funding agency's overall mission and read it carefully. Research past programs they have funded. Determine their current area of focus. Doing this, I found that the year prior to this, the funding agency emphasized "reactive" efforts. Now they've done a 180 and are funding "proactive" services.

Let's consider the above example as if we're a planning team designing a gang/violence prevention counseling program. We know we provide two types of counseling: preventative (before something happens) and intervention (after something happens).

In terms of the RFP's language, what we call preventative is the same as what they refer to as "proactive." What we call intervention is what the RFP calls "reactive."

Once we understand that we both mean the same thing, but that we just label it in a different way, we're able to read between the lines. In this case, the excerpt is telling us that in the balance of services offered, we will be more competitive if we focus on preventative, pre-emptive forms of counseling and education—that is, "proactive."

As I said, it takes a few reads to decipher some of this. But now that we've done the research and read between the lines, it's clearer what they want. Now, our writing will be that much clearer and will more specifically address "the department's overall vision."

The better the reader, the better the writer.

If The RFP "Suggests" It, It's In

If it's important enough for the funding agency to mention in the RFP—it's important enough for you to address in your program design.

For example, an RFP may state something like:

"...involving as many stakeholders as possible (e.g., law enforcement) in the planning process is suggested.

As casually as the example above may appear to be written—and as much as it may be buried in the back pages of the 200-page RFP—that one line gives your Planning Team a critical piece of information. Is stakeholder involvement absolutely required? No. The RFP states that it "is suggested."

But if it's important enough for the funding agency to mention—or even allude to—in the RFP, then consider it something that you MUST mention and address in your response.

So, the example above tells you that your Planning Team needs to:

1) Recruit and involve as many stakeholders as possible in the planning process, and
2) Involve a specific stakeholder.

Guess what potential stakeholder is behind the FIRST door you knock on? That's right, a representative from a local law enforcement agency. Why? Because the RFP mentioned law enforcement as an example.

If the RFP suggests it, it's in.

What Was The Question?

After all this deciphering, reading between the lines, highlighting, aligning and Post-It™ noting, there will still be a long list of unanswered questions and points to be clarified.

That's good. It means you're doing your job as a good reader.

So what kind of questions will arise? That depends on the funding agency, the RFP and your preliminary program design.

For example, I just read through an RFP in preparation for a bidder's conference and jotted down a number of questions that, before our program design can be finalized, will need to be answered.

Here is the first question that came to my mind. The RFP states that we will be:

> "...required to provide services to a minimum of 200 clients."

Does that mean the same 200 in all three years? Or, does that mean a cumulative total of 200 by the end of each year for a total of 600 over three years? The entire budget hinges on clearing up the answer to this question.

Here's another question that came up. The RFP states that we should use a:

"...recognized prevention curriculum proven to work with similar populations."

Recognized by whom? What do they mean by "proven to work?" Do they mean an evidenced-based program that has been scientifically evaluated? Do they mean a program approved by the state department of education? Do they have examples of these programs for review?"

Another question: the RFP states that for the grant to be renewed each year, one outcome must be that:

"students' grade point averages improve by a statistically significant amount."

What exactly is a "statistically significant amount?" Is it improvement by one letter grade? A few points in their GPA? And improve over what period of time? Compared to who, another group of students? From the beginning of the year to the end, or improvement compared to their previous year in school?

✢   ✢   ✢

No doubt, your Planning Team will compile similar questions as you read through the RFP. Where do you get answers to those questions? Most funding agencies frown upon or flatly refuse to answer individual questions over the phone. In their effort to level the playing field they want to ensure that all applicants receive the same information and insight. So, some funding agencies request that you submit the questions in writing. Then they post those questions and answers in a "Frequently Asked Questions" (FAQ) link on their web site.

However, the best place to get answers is where we're headed next. That's right campers: shower, shave, floss, and put on your Sunday best—we're going to a bidders conference!

Chapter 3-6

Bidders Conferences
TO GO OR NOT TO GO

Bidders conferences are generally nothing but a big, fat waste of time and energy— *and you should attend every one you can.*

Before I tell you why, let's hear what MOST naysayers neigh about bidders conferences:

- **"They take up too much time:"** True. Sometimes an entire day or more can be wasted traveling back and forth for a few tidbits of useful information.

- **"You hardly ever get a straight answer:"** True. Staff there usually have their hands or tongues tied—or both. For numerous legal reasons, funding agency staff may have to defer or confer later because they are not allowed to give out certain information. Unfortunately, some staff are so overworked that they are unprepared. In other cases, information is delivered in bureaucratic blather that belies comprehension.

- **"There's seldom any new information:"** True again. At some bidders conferences, funding agency staff basically read aloud what's written in the RFP. And, anyhow, new information appears on the web site where they post FAQs. Or when you do approach staff for new information they respond by saying: "E-mail me when I get back to the office, when it's not so crazy." Then they never respond because it's too close to the submission deadline.

- **"They can be demoralizing:"** Unfortunately, this can be true. It's daunting to see the overwhelming number of applicants you're competing against for grant funds.

- **"They're never held in Hawaii:"** Mostly they're held in some uninviting big brick federal building with a building code that specifically states, "All meeting rooms will offer no view, no fresh air, humming fluorescents, out-of-focus PowerPoints™ and microphones that rudely screech out feedback just when attendees are trying to sneak in their precious afternoon siestas."

Why You Need To Go

A bidders conference—or sometimes called an RFP workshop—is one of a series of regional information sessions hosted by members of and consultants to the funding agency administering the grant. These staff help write and issue the RFPs, read and screen the grant applications, choose the awardees, help implement the grant programs, then monitor and evaluate their operation. Often, experienced program providers and past grant awardees will be on hand to answer questions, provide support and facilitate workshops.

The bidders conference is designed to explain and answer your questions about the RFP and proposed program operations. Usually, the conference staff will walk attendees through the RFP section by section, allowing time for questions and making available other sources of information that will help with your program design and written response. Often, this information is more up-to-date than what's in the grant application package, or is over and above what is available on the funding agency web site.

When funding agencies are in what they call their "road show" mode (i.e., ten different cities/bidders conferences in nine days) they begin to hear patterns of recurring questions that are based on collective misunderstandings of the RFP. They get an idea of what they need to explain better and use the time at these bidders conferences to do so.

Personally, I like attending bidders conferences for several reasons—and it's not because of the free food and beverages.

I always learn—or, I should say, make it a point to learn— at least one piece of crucial information that helps me in the planning and writing process.

I like putting faces with the names of those who develop and monitor the programs from which we are seeking funds.

I like the drive to and from the conferences because it gives me an undistracted opportunity to outline my work in my head.

And, each agency has its own unique requirements for budgets and forms that can be better understood by an in-person explanation.

I also happen to *like* to see the applicants I'm competing against. It gives me great satisfaction and confidence to see my competitors become bored, inattentive, restless, return late from lunch, leap up to take a phone call, leave early—or take the position that they know it all and treat it like a social event. I also delight in them rudely sidetalking among themselves as the speaker at the podium tries to dole out helpful—and often times, critical—information.

By them missing out on an opportunity, I'm gaining an advantage.

Perhaps they do know it all. But more likely, MOST attendees don't have the advantage of knowing the four words—four key words—coined by author Jack London when he was asked to offer advice to young writers wanting to improve their writing.

Four words that, when you read them, will define the approach needed at a bidders conference to take your program design to the next level.

Four words that I'll bet you remember when you go to your next bidders conference.

The four words of advice from Jack London to remember when you attend a bidders conference? Drum roll please...

"Listen With Hungry Ears"

Like reading between the lines of an RFP, valuable information is offered at the bidders conferences, if you listen carefully and eagerly with "hungry ears." Your ears should constantly devour tiny morsels of information that could give your program design an advantage over others.

In every grant application there are programmatic questions with answers that lie somewhere in the gray area because there are no clear cut, right or wrong responses. Explanations of complex issues, specific definitions of imprecise terms and amendments to legislation that fund a program seem to change each year and within each funding agency. It's only after attending bidders conferences and listening with "hungry ears" that your Planning Team can adequately address these gray areas in a way that will make your program design more competitive. Listed below are a few examples:

➤ Minimum Number Of Clients Provided Services

As discussed several times throughout this book, this is always a tough one to answer—and one of the most crucial to your planning process.

Set the number too high and you appear too naïve, ambitious and unable to provide adequate services within the budget limitations.

Set it at too few and the agency will think they won't get enough bang for their buck.

And to make things more difficult, most RFPs don't commit to specifying a number because the answer always varies. But at the bidders conference, you often get an idea if your proposed number to be served is in the ballpark.

➤ How To Count The Number Of Your Clients

Bidders conferences can help you solve the "duplicated" vs. "unduplicated" debate. Does the funding agency use "duplicated service contacts?" As discussed in Chapter 2-3, this means, for example, that if you run a health clinic, every time a person receives a service or referral counts as one contact. So, one client may have 15 service contacts in a year.

Or does the agency use the "unduplicated clients" tally? This means that you count each person served as one, regardless of the number of services they receive.

Of course, these aren't the only formulae. Each agency's methods will differ and each will have different preferences that may not always correlate with what the RFP states—which is another reason to attend bidders conferences.

➤ Evaluation Requirements

The evaluation section of the RFP often seems so cryptically coded by governmental gobbledygook that it fails to provide you (unless you spent five years earning your Masters Degree in evaluation and statistics) with few of the details really necessary to plot out your evaluation design component. Often, this section comes down to your Planning Team asking,

"How do we roll out a competitive $150,000 pie-in-the-sky evaluation plan with our $7,500 evaluation budget?"

So what might you get for answers about evaluation from a bidders conference? You might:

- ✓ Get a better idea of what percentage of the budget should be earmarked for evaluation
- ✓ Learn about preexisting evaluation forms and templates
- ✓ Receive parameters for hiring an external evaluation coordinator

➤ The Latest Research and Data

Many months will have passed between the time the RFP was initially written and the bidders conference. During that time, additional information and data may have surfaced too late to be included in the RFP. So at the bidders conference, you will be supplied with more relevant and topical data in the form of handouts or from funding agency staff presentations. This could include relevant web sites, evaluation report findings, scientifically validated studies, other programs that have been approved and adopted by states, what legislators require in newly funded grant programs and recognition and awards garnered by best practice models. All of this is valuable cutting edge data that, when included in your proposal, is going to help make your program design more valuable and cutting edge.

For example, as I write this I am also working on a Safe Schools/Healthy Families federal grant. When the legislature approved funding for the RFP process and the RFP was written, crime rates (especially those linked to gang-related crimes in inner-city areas) had leveled off. Because of that, our program design was less focused on intervention and more on prevention and education. However, from the time the RFP was written to when our grant proposal was submitted (*a period of nearly 24 months*) crime rates (especially those linked to gang-related crimes in inner-city areas) saw a resurgence. Because of that, we had to rewrite our proposal to address the latest statistical increases in crime and refocus our program design to include more law enforcement intervention activities. By doing this, we not only claimed to be experts in this area, we demonstrated it by citing the latest research and data.

➤ What Constitutes A Legal Agreement

While this may seem like a small detail compared to the enormous task of planning and writing the grant, there's a potential that, at worst, your entire grant can be disqualified because you provided the funding agency with one type of document when they expected another. There are three basic types of agreements to consider here:

✓ **A Letter of Support** is typically written by a community stakeholder (an individual or agency representative) that will not be involved in day-to-day program implementation but will endorse, and vouch for, the program partners. These Letters of Support acknowledge: 1) that the letter writer has reviewed or discussed the proposed program,

2) that the endorser agrees that a critical need for services exists and is not adequately addressed by current resources in the area, and 3) the letter writer is familiar with, and unreservedly endorses, the work done by the lead agency and/or partner agencies within the target community or for similar populations.

✓ A **Letter Of Agreement** is typically written by a partner agency that will be involved in program implementation. This Letter of Agreement: 1) covers the content of the Letter Of Support (detailed above), 2) briefly outlines what the partner agency intends to contribute to the program in terms of services, manpower, in-kind contributions and cash, and 3) what that partner agency understands it will receive from the lead agency in terms of compensation (if any) for services rendered.

✓ A **Memorandum of Understanding (MOU)** is a signed deal memo (an abbreviated, but legal, contractual agreement) between the lead agency and each contractor and partner to be involved. Each RFP/RFA will spell out what details they want in the MOU and usually provide a legal department-approved template to follow.

Some funding agencies see an MOU as just a more elaborate letter of support that state that partner agencies intend to collaborate if grant funds are received. Others see it as a legally binding contract. Find out how the funding agency defines it.

> ### ➤ Specific Budget Questions

Navigating through budget forms and formulae, especially those in federal grants, can often be a dizzying labyrinth. Remember, funding agency representatives at bidders conferences don't just read and award grants, they often monitor the same programs as well. In most cases, they will walk attendees through each category of the budget, often citing invaluable examples of minimum or maximum amounts. For example, this can be especially critical when determining the percentage of administrative costs allowed in your budget.

At bidders conferences, you may discover that a substantial chunk of the budget that you had allocated for program components may need to be earmarked by other requirements from the funding agency. Such items as mandatory evaluation costs, required travel and training expenses, minimum staff qualifications that result in increased wage levels, the required purchase of materials or curricula and more expensive insurance policies are just a few examples. Before you know it, these expenses can eat up 30% of your budget.

> ### ➤ Sustainability

Most funding agencies have different interpretations of sustainability. What can you garner from the conference about sustainability that you can't get from the RFP or off a web site?

Specifics.

Does the funding agency want you to be self-sustaining *by the end* of the grant or be *working toward* that goal? What does "working toward that goal" mean? Do they want you to include clear-cut sustainability goals in your proposal? Again, there's no right answer. But at the bidders conference you can get a clearer idea.

"Not At Liberty..."

Woody Allen's quote, "80% of success is showing up," relates to this section on bidders conferences.

Again, understand that whether it be in their office or at the bidders conference, staff, because of policy, are often "not at liberty" (a favorite phrase of theirs) to dole out information that would give an unfair advantage to one specific bidder.

Here's one way it happened for me at a bidders conference, while trying to get a more specific idea of what their RFP described as:

> "... annual average costs expended per client should be fair and reasonable."

I posed a number of pointed questions to funding agency staff who hadn't given us bidders any kind of yardstick for what was "fair and reasonable."

Knowing that the success of our program design was dependent on getting this clarification of "fair and reasonable," I kept badgering them for a specific example of a program that had "fair and reasonable" costs. It was the classic dog-chasing-its-tail dilemma. I requested they tell us what was "fair and reasonable" and we would then design our program around those parameters. They were standing firm with the idea that we should design a program based on what we thought was "fair and reasonable" then justify the cost. But if the cost was not within what they deemed "fair and reasonable…"—oh well, you get the idea.

The staff's final response? To confer and defer; they were "…not at liberty to give out such information."

Soon after, during a break, realizing I had perhaps hounded them too much in front of the gathering, I approached one of the funding agency staff and apologized. She understood completely. And she hoped that I understood that she was simply not allowed by "the powers that be" to give out any of the numbers I was hounding her for.

No problem. We shook hands. She asked me where I was from and what I was working on and I told her our Little Bit Pregnant Pitch (where have you heard that one before?) about the project, "…and we plan to serve 600 youth per year at approximately $750 per year per youth." As we parted, she again apologized about not being able to give me specific numbers.

But then, with a wry wink and a smile, she said, "…but you're right…in the ballpark."

Earlier, I mentioned that bidders conferences were great for getting an idea if your numbers are "in the ballpark." That reassurance *could only come from me being AT the bidders conference.*

Oh, by the way, we won the grant, which was—and still is—the largest amount ever received by that type of program in the county.

Was there a connection between us winning and that one quick and simple in-person exchange I had with the staff member that verified we were on the right track?

I am "not at liberty to give out such information."

Wearing The Brown Lipstick

"Face time," "meet and greet," "networking," or "wearing the brown lipstick"—however you want to look at it and whatever you want to call it, the example above illustrates how important it is to make personal contact with at least one representative from the funding agency.

But a word of caution, plan on having only a few brief moments of time with agency reps who will no doubt be behind schedule, overbooked and distracted. Don't try to dominate their time and leave them with the feeling that you will have to be surgically removed if they want to get rid of you.

And another word of caution: don't have the audacity to ask these reps for an advantage over others.

I repeat: *Any attempt to cajole or falsely flatter agency representatives is completely unethical and has no place in this business.*

And I say this on behalf of all the hard-working, under-paid, friendly, articulate, well-read, insightful, unselfish and impeccably-groomed funding agency representatives—the same ones who may be reading/scoring *my* grant proposals someday ☺.

In this third section of the book, I saved the best for last—best practice that is. Where do you find these best practice models referenced at bidders conferences? How can you use them to make your program design better? Read on.

Chapter 3-7:

Best Practice Models
"RE-IMAGINING"

A few years ago, a famous movie director of a very famous remake defensively responded to an interviewer who accused him of not being original and, in many instances stealing shot-for-shot, from the original version:

"We didn't steal, we re-imagined."

The director went on to say he took the best parts from the old movie, updated them and fitted them to what worked for his new and updated vision.

In program design, the equivalent of this is studying best practice models and picking the brains of experts in the field.

So if you're going to steal—uh, "re-imagine"—then at least re-imagine from the best.

In fact, studying other successful programs and applying what works for them to your Target Population and situation is perfectly acceptable and, in fact, *expected* of your Planning Team.

Best practice models are those programs funded by the prospective funding agency that have operated successfully over a period of time. Successful, in this case, means that they are exceeding expectations and innovating new ways of delivering program services more effectively and economically.

Best practice models set a standard to which all new and existing programs will be compared.

Experts in the field are those staff on the frontline, operating and advising these best practice programs. Other experts are researchers/evaluators who compare, study and report about these best practice models and work in the area of theory, scholarly reports, policy-making, evaluation and/or textbooks on the subject.

This chapter is about where to find these best practice models and ways to "re-imagine" these models to improve your program design.

Choosing A Model

Also referred to as research-based, scientifically validated or evidence-based models, best practice models have gone through a rigorous, third-party evaluation. Their success has been validated, documented and their methods proven replicable in other settings.

More and more funding agencies, especially federal and state agencies, require that you select from a list of best practice models. If you should choose other then a best practice model, you will need to spend a considerable amount of space in your proposal justifying your decision and the unapproved program you chose. By the way, rarely do these grant applications receive funding.

Keep in mind three factors when choosing a best practice model from an approved list:

1) Find those models that have worked in a similar setting and with a similar target population as yours.

2) You have license to, and in many cases are expected to, adapt the best practice model to your local needs—as long as you stay within the existing framework of the best practice model.

3) Working with a best practice model almost always results in additional costs to your program. This could include: additional training from a short list of approved trainers, required materials, additional evaluation activities, and mandatory staffing requirements.

In terms of program implementation, incorporating a best practice model makes your program more effective and efficient in two ways:

1) Many items such as forms, policies and procedures, evaluation tools, and learning materials have already been created, tested and refined, avoiding the necessity of you starting from scratch.

2) In terms of the grant competition, it levels the playing field between smaller and larger programs/ agencies. Why? Basically a best practice model is

like a brand name. What do you associate with a brand name? A good reputation, reliability, field-testing and the endorsement and backing of experts. When a smaller program/agency associates themselves with a best practice model (i.e., a brand name) they automatically become less of a risk in the eyes of the funding agency.

Where To Find Best Practice Models

Your goal will be to find best practice models that serve a similar target population as yours, in a similar environment (rural, urban, etc.) and within approximately the same budget. Here's where to look:

- **Funding, and federal and state agency, Web sites** (and their regional support centers) that are overflowing with resources and best practice models to support start-up programs in every conceivable aspect of program design, operations and sustainability.

- **In RFPs** where models and experts are referenced in the instructions or in the appendices with contact information, profiles and web site addresses.

- **At bidders conferences** where representatives of best practice models are often asked to conduct workshops, hand out materials and answer your specific questions.

- **Major colleges or universities** that hire experts to conduct evidenced-based evaluations or advise local nonprofit programs.

- **In your community** where you can get a first hand look at a program in operation. These can be found through various city and county government web sites and the community-based organization that runs the program.

- **Funding agency staff** who, if you simply call and ask them for an example of what they consider a top program in your area, will gladly give you several to choose from.

- **In books and textbooks** about the subject area of your proposed program. Often authors will incorporate case studies of best practice models or, at the least, cite several in their bibliography.

- **Private foundations often** commission studies of what works, common issues that need to be addressed by grant programs and trends in program delivery. These are available on their Web sites.

While this book is not about the details of writing a proposal, I will suggest that you briefly describe this research process in your grant application. This will demonstrate that you've done your homework, become knowledgeable about the subject, and are willing to adapt the program to your Target Population's needs. The following example of how I described one such research process is more than what the RFP asked for—but winning grants are chosen because they deliver more than the RFP asks for:

In order to select the school reform model best suited to Generic Unified's Implementation Plan, the Generic Program planning team researched dozens of state and federal school reform models on the Internet. The team also examined school reform models in existing binders of information collected at State Department-sponsored educational conferences. Additionally, the team was extremely fortunate to be linked with Generic University's Dr. Janet Doe (Graduate School Research Center/Educational Leadership and Organizations). Her expertise is in the area of school reform and development, school-family collaboration, and professional development. For the past five years, she has been the principal investigator for a statewide study of the state School Leadership Team Professional Development Program. During this time she also conducted research and evaluation studies of the Program for Parents (PEP) identified by the State Department of Education as a "best practice" model for parent involvement. Based on this research and meetings with Dr. Doe, the planning team concluded that there is no "one-size-fits-all" best practice model that could meet the needs of each subgroup of the Generic Program's target population (i.e., students, teacher, parents and the community). Instead, Dr. Doe assisted the team in drawing elements from three best practice models (as identified by the state) that are most closely aligned with the Generic Program's intervention strategies.

Specific Questions

Every boxer has the perfect strategy to win a fight—that is until s/he is hit for the first time. That old boxing adage holds true for program providers as well. When you've survived this exhaustive program design process, written and submitted the grant and finally win a grant award, you are on top of the world. You swear that you have a flawless model, have thought of everything and that the program will roll out as neatly as the text of your proposal printed on the page.

And then when you begin to implement the program, reality smacks you right in the kisser.

Can you say standing eight count?

The ideals and aspirations of your program design crash headlong into the shortcomings and compromises that any program staff faces in their ramp-up period: the difficulty of recruiting qualified staff, running over budget, facilities falling through, partners disappointing, schedules collapsing, additional funding agency requirements, and dozens and dozens of other mishaps. It happens to everyone.

And like the boxer, the programmers look at each other, as if knocked out on their feet, muttering, "...what just hit us?"

That's why, when you ask specific questions of the best practice model staff, it is not only important to find out what works, but also what doesn't work—and why. Here are a few examples of questions you could ask staff of best practice models:

- ✓ What would they do differently if they were starting-up their program all over again (especially in the areas of budgets, staffing patterns, outreach and training)?
- ✓ What is their most effective ratio of staff to clients?
- ✓ What curriculum (if applicable) do they use? How did they modify it to meet the specific needs of their target population?
- ✓ What is their decision-making process? How does leadership include performance data, staff expertise and client feedback into the decision-making process?
- ✓ What type of training and professional development activities do they find more useful than others?
- ✓ What is their most effective use of volunteers?
- ✓ How have they used evaluation efforts to improve their program on an on-going basis?
- ✓ What is their relationship with the funding agency? What aspects of the program were funding agency program monitors most concerned about? Least concerned about?

✓ How did their *proposed* first year expenditures match up with their *actual* first year expenditures? Would they budget differently? How so?

Don't be shy. As part of the requirements of executing the program as set forth by the funding agency, best practice models are typically mandated to share their successes with upstart programs and disseminate their results to anyone who can use the information.

Also, it's not like these best practice models are in a commercial cutthroat business like soft drinks where formulas and recipes for success are well guarded and billions of dollars in profits are at stake.

Instead, what's at stake is society.

You are talking to non-profit, human service agencies that are in the business of not making a profit but, instead, helping the disadvantaged profit from the services they receive. Staff from these best practice programs are generally very giving, articulate, humble (and humbled) professionals who are flattered that you think enough of them and their programs to inquire. I am often humbled and overwhelmed by their generosity, frankness and eagerness to help in any way they can.

Applying What You've Learned To Your Program Design

You've researched best practice models, interrogated their staff and decided which program elements will work best with your Target Population.

Now, here are a few examples of applying what you've learned from those best practice models into your program design:

✓ **Training:** Allocate part of your budget to hire an expert from their staff to train your staff. Or, ask to use, or pay for, some of their training materials. And in your proposal, base your staff training on their exemplary content and format.

✓ **Curriculum:** Find out what curriculum they use successfully and use it in your program design as a selling point.

✓ **Consultation:** Consider paying one of their staff to serve as a consultant in your start-up year. It sure helps to ride with someone who knows all the bumps down the road. And it's a strong selling point too. Or, invite one of their staff to serve on your Advisory Board.

✓ **Evaluation:** See if you can hire their Evaluation Coordinator for your project. Evaluation Coordinators usually work on multiple projects at the same time so there is no exclusivity factor. Short of that, see if that Evaluation Coordinator or someone on her/his staff will consult with you in the design of your evaluation component. Again, a big selling point in your proposal.

✓ **Proposal review:** Hire one of their staff for a few hours to review a draft of your program design as if they were a Reader/Scorer. They have keen insight into what the funding agency is looking for. Also, chances are they have experience as proposal readers for the funding agency and a trained eye for important details.

Remember that the best implemented programs are usually the result of the best program designs—this is where it all starts.

But even the most successful best practice models, when ramping-up from the page to the street, are like the punch drunk boxer who looked back at his career and said:

"When I was a fighter I kept my head. I lost my teeth, but I kept my head."

Chapter 3-8

Epilogue
PROGRAM DESIGN IN A NUTSHELL

A question I'm often asked is how did a film school brat/television executive/producer-director/screenwriter/screenwriting teacher/radio host end up in the non-profit world designing programs and writing grants that help the disadvantaged?

The question should not be "How...?", but "Why...?"

And my standard answer?

"I have better things to do."

Although I am still involved in stories, creative writing, video production and other forms of media, I was simply not cut out to be in the mainstream of show business. For the brief time I was in the mainstream of show business, I never felt a part of it.

Instead, I felt apart from it.

And remember, I didn't end up pursuing this program design stuff because of a calculated career path or because it was my major in college. Nor did I run around as a six-year old telling everyone I wanted to be a designer of grant programs when I grew up (for the record, my first choice was to become a fire truck and my second choice was to be Jerry Lewis). But, through a cathartic and serendipitous series of job changes, moves, health problems, experiences, friendships, bad breaks and just as many twists of good fortune, I ended up doing what I do now—helping others.

I'm not looking down at anyone else, or up at anyone else. I'm just looking at myself in the mirror. And when I look in the mirror I see someone who can sit at the computer and for every hour he sits there, earn an average of $7,000 for those less fortunate.

Think about that for a moment...

If you knew that you could do the same, how would that change you? What effect would it have on your conscience? How would that change how you use your allotted amount of heartbeats? What kind of moral Jui Jitsu hold would that lock you in? How would your time spent in front of the computer change?

To me it can be boiled down to a quote made famous by Albert Einstein:

> "Try not to become a man of success but
> rather try to become a man of value."

One would assume that the most rewarding aspect of what I do is represented by more than $385 million in grant money for the less fortunate that I've been part of winning.

Or, the fact that the majority of people I work with are true heroes, sacrificing personal goals and better incomes to improve the lives of those less fortunate.

Or, that a program design I worked on in is permanently enshrined in the Smithsonian Institute.

Or, that I am the lead writer of one of the largest and most innovative grant writing firms in the country built on cornerstones of integrity, innovation and mutual respect.

But success is not measured by dollars or prestige alone.

There are other positive residual effects that I value:

- The first senior class of a grant-funded charter high school—established in a community that, at one time, had a 65% dropout rate—graduating 97% of their class, with 85% of those graduates being the first in their family accepted into college.

- A grant-funded field trip for a troop of unlettered parents of two-year-olds visiting a college campus regularly so both the parents and children get the idea that college is part of their future.

- A teacher winning a $1,000 grant for a garden and the day-long class celebration that followed.

- A battered woman stepping into a grant-funded health clinic for the first time, daring to talk to a mental health counselor about breaking the cycle of violence.

- A middle school student greeting me courteously on campus, not because he knows who I am or he has been told to, but because he is applying one of the pillars of a grant-funded district-wide character education program.

That's the "better" in something better to do.

Blazing New Trails

You may recall, from the first chapter, me describing how, when asked, I rarely read someone's proposal. Instead, I ask them to describe their team's design process.

Their most common replies?

What team?

What design?

What process?

This strategizing and thinking about program design is a new frontier. Grant writing is too often thought of as the process of filling in the blanks and cutting and pasting. The thinking goes, when you write one grant you've written them all because it's just a matter of mindlessly cutting and pasting prefabricated answers to standard questions.

I sincerely hope this book will be a step away from this prevailing cut and paste mentality and toward excellent program designs that better serve the less fortunate.

That's not to say that everything in this book is new or invented by me. These are principles and tricks that many top grant writers and program designers carry around in their heads—but seldom do they articulate or share.

Jon's Almost World Famous Seven Cs! are not about reinventing the wheel. They are, however, about helping your Planning Team build a newer and better steering system.

So the purpose of this book is not to transform you into a successful grant writer overnight.

Instead, it is to help you to *think* like a successful grant writer and learn the ability to get your program design right, before you write.

And whatever you do, don't get frustrated and give up.

You will be blazing new trails here, doing some outside-the-box thinking the likes of which you and your Planning Team may have never done before. You will be recalibrating your brains and trying to wrap them around new ideas and new strategies that will eventually lead to greater rewards.

And Much Of The
Battle Is Internal

I often joke in screenwriting class that so much of writing is finding that one special yoga position where you can reach your foot around to give yourself a firm kick in the backside so that you sit down and work at it everyday.

The main thing is to have confidence. To me confidence comes from tirelessly doing your homework and doing right, what you believe is right.

What was it that guy who wore the coonskin cap said? "Be always sure you are right then go ahead."

Remember, if you are on the frontline providing program services to your Target Population, fighting the good fight every day, there is no greater expert about what you do than you.

Also remember, never look at someone else's work and think, "oh I could never do that."

As Howard Gardener's theory states in *Multiple Intelligences*:

> "Do not ask how smart you are,
> ask how you are smart.
> Do not ask how motivated you are,
> ask how you are motivated."

If nothing else about this book you'll remember the rather crude way I started, making the point that when you start with bullshit, no matter how you cut it, paste it, rephrase it, format it, or analyze it—it's still going to be bullshit.

That's why it's important to get it right before you write.

But, as in any group endeavor, getting it right starts with *one person* willing to think in a new way.

So, why not you?

✢　✢　✢

And that's the book in a nutshell—an appropriate receptacle for this business we're in, wouldn't you say?

ACKNOWLEDGEMENTS

I'm often asked, "What have you gained by working for so long and so hard with the people at the Lennox School District?"

My answer: "About 20 pounds."

Seriously, attend any meeting or function within the Lennox School District and you will be greeted with plate after plate of irresistible goodies. And this kindness and generosity is typical of the amazingly tireless, talented, tenacious, forward-thinking professionals who work there in every capacity. I don't think I've ever seen a collection of so many good people do so many good things for the good of others. Fate loves the fearless, I guess. So, my first acknowledgement is to those I so admire at the Lennox School District — the little district that could.

My second acknowledgement goes out to "Darth Edit." You know who you are. What you don't know is how much we appreciate your lightsaber-like precision and your pushing us toward the highest possible standards.

My third and most heartfelt acknowledgement begins with an actual conversation:

Me: Char, seriously, hear me out. I mean with all the work you've done on this book and the fact that we sit here every morning going over every line and every word, I really think we both should be listed as the authors –

Charlotte: No, no, no! It's your book, it's your idea, you've done all the work and you deserve all the credit! I'm just here to do whatever I can to make the book better and help you get it out there so people can read it and use this stuff. I am not the author! Don't mention it again!!!

Typically, I didn't listen. I mention it here again as my feeble way of saying thanks "Y."

Index

access to services, equitable,
194–195
acronyms, program, 209–210
active verbs, 105, 162–164, 167
adversity, character development
and, 49
advisory boards, 185, 189, 192
applications, grant
"Aha!" factor for, 32
competitive scoring of,
15–16, 31
conceptual structure of,
21–33
evaluation of, 15–16, 31
innovative thinking for, 29
program's overarching goals
and, 28
quality of, 16–17, 26, 30
"Readers/Scorers" of,
15–16, 31
statistical data in, 17–18
"underdog" factor in, 27,
66–67. *See also under*
characters.
when not to submit, 35–37
"artfully selling the problem," 25,
90–91
audit history requirements, 255

"backstory," characters', 50. *See*
also under target populations.

baseline data, target populations
and, 70–71
best practice models
choosing, 288–290
locating, 290–291
program design and, 295–297
researching, 290–293
questions for staff and,
293–295
value of, 287–290
bidders conferences
best practice models and, 290
information available at,
277–285
personal relationships built
at, 285–286
value of, 273–277
"Bill of Writes," 21–33, 235
brainstorming sessions
identifying conflicts and,
133–144
program names and, 211–212
budgets, program's, 234–235,
255–256, 282

Campbell, Joseph, 41–42
Cape, Ronald E., 25
cash matches, 197–198, 256
catharses, emotional, 86–87, 155
change
characters', 155–159

crisis and, 157–158
target populations and,
161–177
characters
change in, 155–159
conflicts of, 126–129
crises of, 83–87
development of, 48–50
dimensionality of, 48–50, 156
importance of, 47–52
motivations of, 50
perceptions of, 50
powers of, 49–50
quests of, 99–102, 110–115,
126–129
target populations as, 53–83
transformation of, 52
"underdog," 51–52
collaboration
defined, 182–183
importance of, 181–182
innovation and, 188
mandated by funding
agencies, 190–195
movie making and, 179–180
See also collaborative.
collaborative
advisory boards and, 185, 189
cash matches and, 197–198
cooperation on, 183
defined, 182–183
diversity in, 192
efficiency of, 183–190,
196–197
equal access promoted by,
194–195
evaluation results and,
188–190

financial advantages of,
196–197
formative evaluation and,
188–190
funding gaps mitigated by,
198–199
in-kind contributions and,
197–198
innovation and, 188
lead agencies and, 183–185
local experts on, 199–200
mandated by funding
agencies, 190–195
new programs and, 197
outreach campaigns and,
186–187
target populations and,
191–192
two-way communication of,
193–194
See also collaboration.
colleges, best practice models
and, 290
communication, two-way, 193–194
community based organizations
(CBOs), 183–185
community foundations, 242–243
conflict
brainstorming to identify,
133–144
external, 127–128, 135
extraneous, 145–148
grouping, 149–151
importance in storytelling,
125–129
internal, 128, 135–136
perception and, 139–140
physical, 126–127, 133–134

Index

summarizing, 152–153,
161–165
target population's, 131–154
conjunctive phrases, avoiding,
106, 162, 164
copyright laws, program name
and, 213–214
county grants, 237
crises
causes of, 94–95
catharsis and, 86–87
change and, 157–158
effects of, 97–98
emotional depth and, 85
empirical proof of target
population's, 93–94
defining, 91–93
locality and uniqueness of,
96–97
measuring target population's,
93–94
vs. need indicators, 90
recent occurrence of, 95–96
repercussions of, described,
97–98, 119–120
as storytelling element, 83–87
in target populations, 91–98
criteria, target population
definition and. See need
indicators.
"cuests." See quests.

data
bidders conferences and,
279–280
evaluation results and,
188–190
deadline story clocks, 111–115
deadlines, submissions, 257–259

descriptive elements, target
population definition. See need
indicators.
development notebooks, 234
dimensionality of characters,
48–50, 156
Disney, Walt, 42–43
diversity, collaborative agencies
and, 192
duplicated clients, target
populations and, 70, 278

eligibility requirements
audit history and, 255
cash matches, 256
current funding and, 261–262
deadlines and, 257–259
financial, 255–256
geographic restrictions and,
257
grant guidelines and, 260–261
in-kind matches, 256
non-profit status and, 254–255
odds of success and, 251–254
personal relationships and,
259–260
timeline requirements and,
257–259
emotional response, writing to
produce, 84–87, 155–159
environments, character
developments and, 49
equitable access to services,
194–195
ethics, program design and,
249–250
evaluation coordinators, 296
evaluation results, collaborative
agencies and, 188–190

evidence-based models. *See* best
practice models.
external conflict, 127–128, 135

federal grants, 235–236
formative evaluation, 188–190
Foundation Center, 241
foundation grants, 237, 259
foundations
    best practice models and, 290
    community, 242–243
    foundation grants, 237, 259
    Meet the Grantor Sessions
        and, 243
    open submission dates of,
        259–259
    personal relationships with,
        259–260
funding agencies
    audit history and, 255
    best practice models and,
        288–289
    bidders conferences and,
        274–286
    collaboration mandated by,
        190–195
    eligibility and, 251–262
    deadlines of, 257–259
    evaluation requirements of,
        259, 278–279
    financial requirements of, 255
    geographic restrictions of, 257
    government agencies as,
        198–199, 235–237
    grant size and, 252–253
    honesty with, 90–91
    invitations to apply, 238–239
    lead agencies and, 184–185

legal agreements and, 280–282
non-profit status and,
    254–255
personal relationships with,
    259–260
pitching to, 223–229
portion of population served
    and, 68–69, 277–278
program's fit with, 247–262
programs funded by,
    260–262, 267
reporting requirements of,
    259
RFPs of, 71–73, 235, 238–239,
    266–272
timetables of, 120–121,
    257–259
Web sites of, 239–240
writing to match vision of, 24
See also funding sources,
    researching.
funding sources, researching
    fee-based resources for, 245
    invitations to apply and,
        238–239
    locating sources and, 239–245
    system for, 231–235
    See also funding agencies.

gaps in services, identifying,
    136–139
geographic distribution of funds,
    253
geographic restrictions, 257
goals
    conflict summaries and,
        161–165
    measurability of, 107, 162, 164

numbering of, 174–176
objectives and, 166–176
program's overarching, 28,
103–107, 118–119
repercussions of not meeting,
119–120
target populations'
overarching, 103, 131–132,
139–141, 145, 152–153, 161
urgency for funding and,
118–119
Goldman, William, 3
Gourgouris, Cheryl, 183
government grants, 235–237
governmental tax-exempt
organizations, 254
grant guidelines, eligibility
requirements and, 260–261
grant responses, structuring, 5
grant writing workshops, 243–244
grant writers
as program designers, 11
role on planning teams, 10–14
grants.gov, 240

impending events, story clocks,
111
indicators, need
vs. crises, 90
defining target populations
and, 57–67, 90
primary, 72–73
secondary, 72–73
in-kind contributions, 197–198,
256
innovation, collaboration and, 188
internal conflict, 128, 135–136
inverted pyramid approach,
program design, 12

Kazan, Elia, 48
knowledge-sharing, non-profits
and, 244–245

lead agencies
collaboratives and, 183–185
eligibility requirements and,
254–255
financial soundness of, 184
as liaison for funding agency,
184
non-profit status requirements
of, 255
letters of agreement, 281
letters of inquiry (LOI), 239
letters of support, 280–281
libraries, researching grants
at, 244
"little bit pregnant" pitches,
225–229
ListServs, researching on, 240–241
local experts, on planning teams,
9–10
logos, program, 209

marketing, social, 186–187
McBain, Ed, 203
measurability
of crisis's extent, 93–94
of objectives, 167–169,
171–172
of overarching goals, 107, 162,
164
qualitative vs. quantitative,
168
Meet the Grantor Sessions, 243
memorandums of understanding
(MOU), 281–282
mores, conflict and, 127–128

"MOST" planning teams, 15
motivations, characters', 50. *See
also under* target populations.

names, program
    choosing, 210–221
    importance of, 203–204
need indicators
    vs. crises, 90
    defining target populations
      and, 57–67, 90
    primary, 72–73
    secondary, 72–73
No Child Left Behind law, 123
non-profits
    non-profit status requirements
      and, 254–255
    knowledge-sharing among,
      244–245

objectives
    goals and, 166–176
    measuring, 167–169, 171–172
    numbering, 174–176
    realistic, 167–169
    specific, 166, 170
    writing of, 166–176
on-line submissions, 257
open submission dates, 257–259
"Or Else" factor
    in program design, 119–120
    in screenwriting, 111–114
    See also under target
      populations.
outreach campaigns, 186–187

"packaging" in movies, 179–180.
    See also collaboration;
    collaborative agencies.

perception
    character's, 50
    conflict and, 139–140
    of target populations, 62–64,
      139–140
personal relationships, building
    at bidders conferences,
      285–286
    with foundations, 237,
      259–260
    with funding agencies,
      259–260, 285–286
physical conflict, 126–127,
    133–134
planning team approach
    "MOST" planning teams
      and, 15
    program design, 9–19
    responsibilities of planning
      teams in, 13–15
    writing process and, 23–33
plot vs. structure, 45
points of view
    characters', 50
    target population's, 62–63,
      139–140
    See also perception.
population profiles. *See* need
    indicators.
powers, characters', 49–50
primary need indicators, in RFPs,
    72–73
program design
    best practice models and,
      295–297
    ethics and, 249–250
    funding agency's fit with,
      247–262
    importance of, 5–7

inverted pyramid approach
to, 12
planning team approach to,
9–19
structural elements of, 21–33,
43–45. *See also* structure.
program designers, grant writer's
role as, 11
program names
choosing, 210–221
importance of, 203–204
proposal reviews, 296–297
public charities, 254

quests
characters', 99–102, 110–115,
126–129
overarching goals as, 103–107
main, overarching, 101–102
story clock and, 110–114

"Readers/Scorers" of applications,
15–16, 31
urgency for funding and,
121–122
regional grants, 237
reporting requirements, 259
Request for Applications/Funding
(RFA/RFF), 238
Request for Proposal (RFP)
best practice models and, 290
evaluation requirements of,
278–279
funding agency's, 71–73, 235,
238–239, 266–272,
highlighting, 265–266
importance of reading,
263–264

primary need indicator and,
72–73
researching grants and, 238
secondary need indicators
and, 72–73
workshops. *See* bidders
conferences.
writing of, 264–265
research-based models. *See* best
practice models.
risk factors, target population
definition. *See* need indicators.
"Running Clocks," 111

sacrifices, character development
and, 50
scientifically-validated models. *See*
best practice models.
screenwriting. *See particular*
screenwriting element.
service marks, program names
and, 213–214
services, gaps in, 136–139
single need indicators, in RFPs,
72–73
slogans, program names and, 208
social marketing, 186–187
solutions, avoiding mentioning,
106, 162, 164
staff-to-client ratios, target
populations and, 69
state grants, 236
statistical data, effective use of,
17–18
story clocks
defined, 109–110
deadline, 111–115
in program design, 117–124

realistic timelines and,
120–121
types of, 111
See also under target
populations.
storytelling
change and, 155–159
characters and, 47–52
conflict and, 125–129
crises and, 83–87, 89–98
levels of, 85–86
quests and, 99–102
story clocks and, 109–115
structure and, 41–45
target populations as
characters and, 53–83
structure
change and, 155–159
characters and, 47–52
conflict and, 125–129
crises and, 83–87, 89–98
plot vs., 45
quests and, 99–102
story clocks and, 109–115
storytelling and, 41–45
writing and, 2–5, 21–33,
39–45
submissions deadlines, 257–259
sustainability, 282–283

tangibility of character quests,
100–101
target areas
borders defined for, 73–75
crises made local for, 96–97
demographic/socio-economic
factors of, 77–78
physical conflicts of, 133–135
risk factors of, 77–79

size of, 76–77
target populations and,
73–79, 96–97
target populations
"backstory" of, 63
baseline data on, 70–71
change and, 161–177. *See also*
change.
characteristics of, 61–67
as characters, 53–83. *See also*
character.
collaborative agencies
and, 191–192. *See also*
collaboration; collaborative
agencies.
communication with,
193–194
conflicts identified for,
131–154. *See also* conflict.
crisis and, 91–98, 104–105.
See also crises.
defining, 57–67
descriptions of, 79–80
determining, 54–57, 71–73
equitable access for, 194–195
gaps in services for, 136–139
motivations of, 64–65.
See also motivations,
characters'.
need indicators of, 57–61, 90
number to receive services,
67–73, 277–278
objectives for, 166–176
"Or Else" factor for, 120
overarching goals of, 103,
131–132, 135, 139–141, 145,
152–153, 161, 166–176
perception and, 62–64

program name reflecting,
207–208, 213
quests and. *See above*
overarching goals of.
social marketing for, 186–187
target areas and, 73–79,
96–97
story clock concept for, 120.
See also story clocks.
as "underdogs," 27, 66–67
tax-exempt charitable
organizations, 254
timeline requirements, 257–259
trademarks, program names and,
213–214
"Type-L" personalities, 30

unduplicated clients, target
populations and, 70, 278
universities, best practice models
and, 290

verbs, active, 105, 162–164, 167

Web sites
best practice models and, 290
researching grants on,
239–240, 244–250
workshops, grant writing, 243–244
writing process
change and, 155–159
characters and, 47–52
conflict and, 125–129
quests and, 99–102
story clocks and, 109–115
story telling elements in,
41–45
structure and, 2–5, 21–33,
39–45

year-round submission dates,
257–259

Eye Hear Ya!

Reader, eye think this is the beginning of a beautiful friendship. But eye need to hear from you. So let me hear your success stories. Use Jon's Almost World Famous Seven Cs! and there will be success stories — oh yes, there will be success. Visit us at:

www.SandyPointInk.com
or contact us at:
P.O. Box 6847, Santa Barbara, CA 93160
(Toll free) 866/674-5222; info@SandyPointInk.com

Get more tips! Swap stories! See examples of winning proposals! Learn about workshops! Find out about new books from Sandy Point Ink! Share your success with others! Learn more ways to win more money for your worthy cause!

Sandy Point INK